SMOOTH SCALING

SMOOTH SCALING

20 Rituals to Build a Friction-Free Organization

ROB BIER

WONDERWELL

Library of Congress Control Number: 2023910928

ISBN 978-1-63756-039-6 (hardcover)

ISBN 978-1-63756-042-6 (EPUB)

Cover design: The Book Designers

Interior design: Adrian Morgan

Author photograph: Nydia Hartono

Published by Wonderwell in Los Angeles, CA

www.wonderwell.press

WONDERWELL

Printed and bound in Canada

To my children, Ava and Nate. Go get 'em.

Table of Contents

Introduction

˅

FOR THE PAST TWELVE YEARS, I've coached the executive teams of start-ups, scale-ups, and larger entrepreneur-led businesses. Before that, I was an entrepreneur and a venture capitalist (VC), so I've seen the challenges that leaders of high-growth companies face from every angle.

Since my time as a VC some twenty years ago, our understanding of how to build businesses has grown dramatically—particularly when it comes to topics such as raising capital, achieving product-market fit, and developing go-to-market strategies. But one aspect remains a common and mysterious challenge for many founders and CEOs: the question of how to build a high-performance organization that scales.

An Unmistakable Pattern

When I started down this path, I didn't expect to write a book about it. But over the years, I noticed that my clients kept encountering the same problems over and over as they grew, often at roughly the same stages in the scaling process—problems like functional leaders whose growth doesn't keep pace with their departments; teams that get bogged down by internal conflicts; cross-functional relationships that become strained or break down entirely; and staff who become disconnected from the company's leadership and devolve into tribes.

Many CEOs ignore these issues—until the problems are severe enough to visibly slow them down. At that point, they

1

tend to approach each symptom as a one-off, trying ad hoc solutions that might help temporarily but don't address the root causes. Others just push harder, throwing more money and people at the areas that are holding them back.

Unsurprisingly, none of these approaches work. The harder you push an organization that's bogged down in friction, the more dysfunctional it gets. This is not exactly a failure of your leadership. What you did in the early days may have worked great, but it won't necessarily work forever.

To be a truly great founder/CEO, you need to be able to not only spot these problems quickly but also anticipate them—and build the habits and skills that enable your organization to avoid them. It's completely doable, but most leaders aren't equipped with the knowledge they need. As a result, many successful scale-ups end up stumbling just as they seem to be coming into their own.

This book is designed to help you avoid that fate.

**The harder you push an organization
that's bogged down in friction,
the more dysfunctional it gets.**

The Missing Framework

The founders I work with are an impressive bunch. As of today, six of my clients have become unicorns during the time I've worked with them. One became a decacorn. They achieved this not because they're super experienced but because they're learning machines, quick to figure out challenges as they arise. And figure it out, they do. How?

Google.

It's a great way to learn. Assuming your question is reasonably well defined, a quick search will often lead you to much of what you need. If the topic lends itself to clear step-by-step instructions—for example, raising capital or implementing objectives and key results (OKRs)—then you'll be able to apply what you learn to your business and generate real outcomes.

But learning to build a high-performance, scalable organization doesn't follow this pattern. It's impossible to master this by reading blogs or watching YouTube videos. The topic is too wide, the boundaries too unclear. We don't even have a clear definition of *high performance*. To some people, it means getting stuff done and nothing more. Others focus on weak or lagging proxies, such as revenue growth, valuation benchmarks, or employee engagement metrics.

The reality is that building a high-performance organization is a multifaceted challenge. If you do research the topic, you'll find plenty of what I call piece parts: advice on specific skills such as how to give feedback, craft your company values, interview candidates, or run a daily stand-up. While these are all useful skills, they don't get to the heart of what makes a scalable, high-performing organization.

Plus, there's a massive philosophical divide running through all the advice on organization and culture. On one side are those who see organizations as complex machines—a set of people and teams that need to be structured and "programmed" to maximize their output. On the other side are those who see organizations as communities—groups of people who need to be nurtured, brought together, and shaped into a cohesive whole with a strong sense of shared purpose and values. It's a confusing world of conflicting advice.

Without a unifying framework, founders find themselves playing Whack-a-Mole, reacting to a never-ending stream of organizational and people problems. They can't see the challenges coming around the corner, or how all the different problems are interconnected. And they often fall into the trap of picking one side of the philosophical divide, ending up with a company culture that is badly lopsided.

This book gives you that unifying framework. It's not a collection of piecemeal advice on how to deal with people problems. It's also not an encyclopedia that covers everything you need to know about HR or growing a business. There are plenty of topics I won't cover here because (1) most companies I encounter already get them right, (2) plenty of useful advice has already been written about them, or (3) they're not game changers for performance. That list includes things like articulating your mission and vision, implementing OKRs, and implementing various types of systems.

Instead, this book presents a unified approach to building a high-performance organization that can scale without limits—without getting bogged down by friction.

What You're About to Learn

In chapter 1, we'll look at what makes scaling so hard, especially after you pass a certain size. In chapter 2, we'll explore what it really means to be a high-performance organization in concrete terms that you can see, feel, and measure. Chapter 3 is where we learn what underpins sustainable high performance: consistently great interactions between your people. Everything you learn in the rest of the book will be in pursuit of that holy grail.

In chapter 4, you'll learn the secret to mastering the skills your organization needs: rituals. Rituals are specific, memorable, easy-to-learn skills that help you—and everyone else in your organization—master and spread the behaviors that prevent friction and sustain high performance. They're the squats and lunges of organizational fitness. In chapter 5, I'll share some tips on how to get the most out of the book and how to get started on your fitness routine.

In chapters 6 through 11, we'll explore the key rituals as they relate to the different types of interactions that take place in your organization, starting with the simplest interaction: two colleagues problem-solving together. We'll start with the rituals that are foundational for any organization, including smaller companies, and work our way toward those that apply mainly to larger companies.

In chapter 12, we'll focus on the most important players in all of this: you, the founder/CEO. As your business grows, your role changes profoundly, and it can be a struggle to keep pace. You'll learn about the key transformations that all CEOs need to go through, when they need to happen, and what it takes to master them—as well as what to do if you can't.

In chapter 13, you'll learn how to architect your organization so that the right interactions happen at the right time, using tools like organizational and meeting design.

The rituals you'll learn throughout the book are the keys to turning this framework into tangible results. They aren't a laundry list of check-the-box actions. They're ways of working that, once you've learned them, integrate seamlessly into what you and your team are already doing every day, replacing the old ways that became problematic. Each one requires a conscious effort to learn and master, but if you stay diligent, they quickly become habits that you perform without thinking about them.

As these rituals spread through your organization, they'll become the default way of doing things. New employees will pick them up naturally by observing their colleagues, so the good habits will scale virally with your organization.

What you'll find in these pages is simply this: a clear guide to understanding, preventing, and eliminating the organizational frictions that make scaling painful and prevent scale-ups from sustaining high performance.

You may be an early-stage founder who's just starting to grow your team and looking for some direction. If so, this book will help you create the organization of your dreams and avoid a whole lot of the pain that most start-ups go through.

If you're further down the road, you're probably already feeling the pain of friction, but all is not lost. Most of my clients are in that boat, and they've all made huge progress. By spreading the rituals across your top team, you'll develop a network of role models who can carry the change from your office through to every employee.

So, if you're ready to build your frictionless business, let's get started.

Chapter 1

The Struggle
to Scale

▼

In this chapter, you'll learn what makes scaling so hard and why the organizational challenges that growth brings take leaders by surprise. You'll also learn about four key inflection points you need to be prepared for.

AS A LEADER IN A HIGH-GROWTH COMPANY, you're obsessed with getting stuff done. Perhaps if you were an executive in a mature enterprise, you could sign off at six o'clock every day, knowing that you have a solidly functioning operation with stable processes and experienced teams—a machine that will do what you need it to most days of the year.

But that's not the path you've chosen for yourself. The idea of being a steward who steers a big, well-run tanker never appealed to you. No, you've always wanted to be a builder—to create something new and better—a business that is faster and nimbler and delivers more customer value than the ones you see around you. This is no stewardship job; it's a *doing* job—and it seems to take ten times as much work. You've had to develop entirely new technologies and get them to work, attract new customers and persuade them to give you a shot, and find new business models and tweak them until they are sustainable. Throughout this period, you've also had to spend time securing investments, whether from venture capitalists or internally if you're part of a larger company. And there are plenty of stakeholders you need to keep on your side.

As your organization has grown and you've brought in better and more experienced people, your job has naturally evolved from getting stuff done yourself to organizing and overseeing the managers and teams that get stuff done. There was once a time when you imagined that all this leverage would enable you to get more control over your time so that you could see your family more or have a healthier lifestyle. But, in fact, the opposite has been the case. You have had to keep a close hand in all the key business areas, and on top of that, you've discovered something a little counterintuitive: the more people you have, the more time you have to spend managing them and dealing with the never-ending stream of organizational tensions that seem to crop up each day.

Your business continues to do well and is poised to grow quickly for some years to come, but perhaps now is the time to ask yourself this question: Am I really on a sustainable path?

Are You Scaling? Or Are You Just Growing?

One key message I hope you'll take from this book is this: growing your head count—or your revenues—is not the same thing as scaling. I'm not sure how many CEOs really appreciate the difference. During the recent period in which money was nearly free, "blitzscaling" and hypergrowth became the venture capital community's favored strategy. The advice given to CEOS was "grow as fast as possible. Use your high growth rate to justify a high valuation. Use the high valuation to support a huge capital raise. And use all that capital to hire as many people as you need and spend as much as you need on marketing to maintain the hypergrowth." This works for venture capitalists because if it leads to a single breakthrough success, it pays off.

Growing your head count—or your revenues—is not the same thing as scaling.

But the reality is that the formula rarely works—and it creates a lot of internal problems. It's true that in a few very specific types of businesses it works well, but many of those who have pushed this thinking have either been disingenuous or sloppy in their thinking. Here's where it does work and, indeed, where it makes perfect sense:

- When you're in a business with overwhelming first-mover advantages. Typically, these are businesses with network effects.

- When you're in a business that is effectively pure software so that you can grow your customer base by 10x or 100x without needing to build physical operations, such as manufacturing, fulfillment, supply chain, customer service, etc.

- When you already know that your business model works and has viable economics.

If you're lucky enough to be leading a business with all those characteristics, congratulations. But the reality is that very few make the cut. The rest of us have to build our businesses one step at a time. We have to constantly improve the quality of all aspects of our product and service as we grow. We also have to build high-performance, cost-effective organizations—otherwise we won't survive. In short, we have to not only *grow* our businesses but also *scale* them.

Over the past twelve years, I've seen many companies pursue the blitzscaling strategy—typically with the strong encouragement of their investors—and the results have not been pretty. Yes, they became big. Quite a few of them achieved unicorn status. But in many cases, the quality of their products or services suffered—particularly when the business relied on some physical operations as opposed to pure bits and bytes. So, high growth led to equally high customer churn.

But most striking is how the quality of their people organizations has been impacted. They all started out with small, committed, highly aligned and high-performing teams. Today they typically employ between five hundred and five thousand employees. This is still a small number compared to a traditional enterprise, yet their organizations are marked by all the dysfunctions of much larger, staler companies: politics, duplication of activities, conflict, bureaucracy, bottlenecks, lack of accountability, and silos.

As a result of these dysfunctions, they're neither efficient nor effective.

Making the Shift

The first time I met Amelia Stanton, she was buzzing with energy. No wonder: she'd recently been hired as the chief human resources officer of Corality, an e-commerce tools provider in Australia, and she'd been charged with growing the staff from three hundred people to more than three thousand over the next five years to support the stellar top-line growth the company was experiencing.

I'd been introduced to her by a mutual friend and offered my help, but at first, she didn't see the need. She had a clear plan, which was to focus on the basics: expanding their talent acquisition team and equipping it with better tools and processes, upgrading the company HR information system, ensuring there were clear policies and processes, and providing enough HR business partners to support all the growing departments.

But when she called me back three months into her new job, this is what she said:

> Corality reminds me of a market I visited in Marrakesh a few years ago: there is a ton of energy, with people running around interacting with each other, but it's all super chaotic. Different departments have different ways of working. Some are into holding lots of meetings, while others do everything on Slack. Conflicts are brought to my attention all the time. I would say that many teams are operating in silos. Individually, our people are excellent, but I feel like we're lacking a framework for how to work together.
>
> We've had the blessing and the curse of too much capital. The result is that our leaders view hiring more people as their go-to solution for every problem. But I realize that we're only making the chaos worse! I feel like we're trying to build a huge jigsaw puzzle by throwing more and more pieces into the box instead of thinking about how they will fit together to create the picture we want.

For the next two years, Amelia and I worked together to implement the rituals that this book describes. Here's how she sees the situation today:

Looking back, I realize that we were growing, not scaling. We were just getting bigger. I see now how quickly that can become messy. It's like those Asian cities that grow fast without planning—they get ugly, congested, and tangled. It felt like we were turning into Bangkok— dynamic but chaotic—but I wanted to build something more like Singapore—smooth, efficient, and low stress.

When we started to talk to the leaders and managers about building a truly scalable organization, instead of just growing numbers, a lot of them had no idea what we meant. Only when we introduced some basic measures of organizational effectiveness did the penny start to drop. Once I could show them that their organizations weren't performing all that well, I came up with a simple rule of thumb: every time they wanted to hire more people, they also had to show me their plans to make their teams and departments function better as they grew bigger. How would they improve team dynamics? Strengthen management? Break down silos?

As we introduced the rituals, they started to see that if they slowed down a little, took time to build the foundations of healthy relationships and interactions within and across their teams, when they added more people to their teams, it actually created more output—not more friction!

Looking at Corality today, we're far from perfect, but there's a real synergy that was missing before. The most important thing is that people trust each other. As a result, managers are finding it easier to manage their people, teams communicate better, and silos, though they still crop up, get dealt with.

When you successfully scale an organization, it also gets bigger, but its culture and performance should stay the same . . . or get even better.

Scaling has become a trendy word for *growing*, but it means something different, something more specific. When you scale something, you make it bigger while preserving its key characteristics. If an image is scaled correctly, it should keep the same colors, proportions, and sharpness as the original—but be bigger. When you successfully scale an organization, it also gets bigger, but its culture and performance should stay the same . . . or get even better.

That doesn't happen by default. If your company is still very small, you could be forgiven for thinking that it does. You may feel that your team is working fantastically together right now: everyone is productive, committed, and happy to be there; collaborations are smooth; decisions get made quickly; and that all seemed to come about fairly naturally. But this early success can easily lull you into a false sense of confidence. It's natural to assume that your small high-performing team will organically grow into a large high-performing team and that your focus should continue to be on getting stuff done—driving the day-to-day growth of the business.

But that would be a mistake.

Why? Because as organizations grow, they tend to get in their own way. Decision-making slows down. Conflicts emerge. Meetings grow longer, less focused, and less productive. Silos develop. Managers spend more of their time handling people and organizational issues and less on business opportunities. In short, *friction* has begun to slow your company down.

Why does this happen?

To understand this, let's look at what I call a Day Zero organization. To illustrate the concept, I'll use a start-up, but it could just as well be a new team or department in an existing company. As with all the narratives in this book, this one is based on real-world clients, but the names of companies and individuals have been changed. In many cases, the narratives represent a composite picture drawn from several companies.

Day Zero at OptiRoute

"Our first year at OptiRoute was just awesome." That's Dr. Arthur Chen talking, cofounder and CEO. Arthur had pulled together a small team of engineers and data scientists to commercialize the AI models he'd developed while doing his PhD. The company was formed to apply these to the transportation industry, focusing initially on trucking. Arthur knew he had the makings of a star team when he convinced his fellow doctoral candidate Julia Perez to run engineering and his old friend Michael Hughes to run product.

Starting out with just a few other people, they worked tirelessly. At first, they didn't even have an office—they mostly worked out of Arthur's dining room in Austin, Texas, or at a local coffeehouse. Fueled by adrenaline and caffeine, they often worked twelve- or fourteen-hour days. Nothing seemed to get in the way of getting work done. Everyone knew what everyone else was working on, how the different parts should come together, and who to ask if they needed help. There was no "us" and "them," no factions or even departments, just one unified team of people inspired by a common mission. Everyone was fresh, energized, and pumped.

Communications happened in a flash—they would just grab the right people and find a spot to talk. When there were tough choices to make, Arthur would invite everyone to sit in his living room and talk it through—these sessions usually took about two hours. But because all the relevant people were involved, there was no need to explain to anyone else the rationale or implications of those decisions—people just got to work implementing them.

Yes, there were frequent disagreements—particularly between Julia's team, which wanted to build a robust scalable tech stack, and Michael's, which wanted to move faster to get a prototype out to the market—but the two teams found they could usually work out a solution over late-night burritos and a few beers.

In short, like many Day Zero organizations, OptiRoute started out *frictionless*.

Soon, the company was beating its milestones, and Arthur's investors were encouraging him to raise more money to grow faster. Of course, he still had plenty of business challenges. For one thing, he hadn't counted on how long it took to persuade customers to get on board, even when the pilot was free. Then he ran into legal issues with his old university about ownership of the IP. Plenty of things got in the way of overnight success, but his people organization wasn't one of them.

Sadly, it didn't stay that way. During the second year, the business started to accelerate. After closing a sizable new round of investment, Arthur and the team went on a major hiring spree. Soon there were over thirty engineers, a dozen in sales and marketing, and a stream of new folks joining other departments.

The rapid hiring was driven partly by the launch of their second product, which focused on air cargo. Arthur hired Terry Pearce from FedEx, who brought some of his team with him. Terry couldn't move his family, so OptiRoute now had two offices: one in Austin and one in Memphis.

Arthur had always been ambitious, and he told everyone who would listen that he intended to build a really big business. He also liked to say that new joiners were force multipliers, people who would translate their vision into an industry-leading company. And, in the early days, new hires were just that—force multipliers who slotted in, understood what needed to be done, and got to work.

But with the addition of each new hire, product, location, and department, the complexity of the OptiRoute organization grew. Arthur didn't see this as a problem . . . until he did. Around the time they reached one hundred people, he started to hear more and more complaints: about how long it took to get decisions made, about resource conflicts, about the amount of time spent in never-ending meetings. But the moment the problem came into focus for him was when his cofounder Julia said they used to ship new product faster when the company was half the size it was now—and Michael agreed.

Friction had reared its ugly head. The magical qualities of Arthur's Day Zero organization were gone.

No leader ever expects their organization to reach this point—because it sneaks up on them. The more successful your business, the faster you grow. The faster you grow, the more time you need to spend on building product, winning new customers, keeping old customers happy, fixing bad code, and hitting targets and deadlines. Growth feels good internally and looks good externally, so it's easy to take pride in your success and ignore the growing frictions. But unless you tend to them, they eventually slow your company down and undermine its performance.

What Was So Right . . . and What Goes Wrong

In a Day Zero organization, everything just *seems to work*. So, what exactly is going on here, and how can you recapture or retain that magic in a much larger organization? Let's go back and examine what made OptiRoute so effective in its early days.

1. Everyone Knew and Trusted Each Other

Arthur started out with two cofounders he'd known for a very long time. That meant they naturally trusted each other more than if he'd hired executives he didn't know. They could be very direct with each other, disagreeing or giving tough feedback, but they never questioned each other's support. The seeds of a culture were already being sown.

As early hires trickled in, they rapidly picked up on that culture. Long hours, shared meals, and bad jokes brought the team close as they worked to figure out their new business. Familiarity bred trust, which in turn meant that new joiners soon felt safe to share feedback, challenge decisions, and ask awkward questions. Somehow, the more they did this, the more trust they felt.

But as the team grew larger still, it wasn't possible for everyone to get equally well acquainted. Relationships no longer grew by default. Michael was excellent at encouraging people to spend time with and get to know each other on a personal level, but the other leaders didn't emphasize this. Once Terry and his Memphis-based team joined, people stopped assuming that they could have a personal relationship with everyone and focused on the work.

2. People Knew What Was Going On

In a Day Zero organization, there's no confusion about who is working on what or who to go to when you need information or a decision. As a result, communication, coordination, and decision-making happen naturally and effectively, without any formal design.

But as the company took on more people, projects, and especially locations, it became impossible for everyone to know all that was going on or who was responsible for what. There were lots of trade-offs to be made about resource allocation and prioritization. The more complex the organization became, the more people brought these questions and decisions to Arthur because he was the only one with the entire organizational overview. But he soon became a bottleneck.

3. Everyone Felt Part of a Single Team

When people joined OptiRoute in the early days, they didn't really join a department or team—they joined the company, and that's where their loyalties lay. Luckily, the culture at OptiRoute kept people feeling that way for a long time—but at the point that Arthur launched the air cargo business, it started to change.

By that time, the original trucking team was generating revenues and had demanding targets—so they felt they should have first call on any shared resources. But the air cargo business was still in prototype. Terry needed lots of support from the engineering and data science teams in Austin, but as a newcomer, he didn't get the level of support and responsiveness he felt he should have, and his team grew frustrated. Over time, this evolved into an "us and them" subculture. Not long after that, Arthur heard someone say that "those damn guys in Memphis are always griping"—a wake-up moment that something was wrong.

4. Colleagues Learned How to Work with Each Other

With the intensity of working side by side all day and into the evening, it didn't take long for people to figure out each other's personalities, strengths, quirks, and preferred ways of working. Julia was detail oriented, wanted things in writing, and insisted others do the same. Arthur wanted to hear creative ideas about how the product could be better and was happy to spend hours brainstorming at a whiteboard. Hasan, an early engineering hire, needed things explained carefully, but once he got it, his productivity was off the charts.

But as the company grew, people increasingly worked with folks they didn't know well. As Julia's engineering department rapidly outstripped the others in terms of head count, her meticulous approach and insistence on documentation soon became the dominant way of working. Others just had to fit in.

5. Priorities and Incentives Were Aligned

OptiRoute's Day Zero team had no confusion about what needed to be done. The company's must-win battles were as clear as could be, and everyone knew what their role was in accomplishing these.

Later, as the company grew, things became less clear. In response, Otto, the HR director, introduced OKRs—and decided that executives' performance should be assessed in part based on their OKRs. Although in theory this may have been a good way to align departmental priorities, in practice things changed too quickly. Soon, most employees had far more clarity about their own department's priorities than they did the company's.

I could keep going. Day Zero organizations have many advantages that are largely the result of being small, but because they occur naturally, we tend to take them for granted. What causes these advantages to slip away, and why do leaders of high-growth companies rarely see it coming? One simple fact: *Head count grows linearly, but organizational complexity grows exponentially.*

Complexity Comes All of a Sudden

As your organization grows, it adds people one at a time. But the complexity of your organization doesn't grow linearly; it grows exponentially. For example, if you have three employees, there are three possible pairs for one-on-one conversations and only one possible combination for a three-way discussion. When you add a fourth employee, you don't just add one more possible pair, you add three! By the time you have thirty people, there are 435 possible two-person pairings and more than four thousand possible groupings of three!

The complexity of your organization doesn't grow linearly; it grows exponentially.

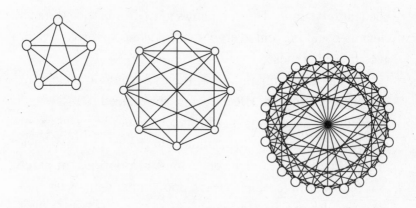

Figure 1.1. A five-person organization, a nine-person organization, and an eighteen-person organization.

This mathematical fact underpins the organizational challenges that all growing businesses face, and it explains why things like communication, coordination, and decision-making become problematic so much sooner than we might expect. More people means more viewpoints, more disagreements, more chances for misunderstandings, more meetings.

And it means more relationships to be built. In short, *managing a growing organization is an exponential problem.*

It's also a neurological problem. In a Day Zero organization, relationships grow naturally and organically, and as new people are hired, new relationships get formed. But human beings can't maintain an infinite number of relationships. In fact, it turns out that the limit on meaningful human relationships is about 150, according to research by Robin Dunbar, a professor of anthropology and psychology at Oxford. This so-called Dunbar's number shows up in all kinds of interesting places:

- It's the average number of guests invited to weddings in the United States.
- It's the most common size of traditional hunter-gatherer tribes.
- It's the average number of recipients on family Christmas-card lists.
- It's the average size of an Amish community.

Even on social media, where people often have hundreds of friends, research conducted by Dunbar showed that most had meaningful relationships with just about 150 of their contacts.[1]

Once your organization reaches this size, you can expect things to start to change. Increasingly, people don't know each other. That's fine; not everyone needs to. But without some deliberate attention, you're likely to end up with gaps where you need strong relationships—and by the time that's apparent, it's often too late.

---

[1] R. I. M. Dunbar, "Do Online Social Media Cut Through the Constraints That Limit the Size of Offline Social Networks?" *Royal Society Open Science* 3, no. 1 (January 2016), doi.org/10.1098/rsos.150292.

On top of that, the quality of your people's relationships changes. In the early days, team members are like comrades, fighting against the odds for a business they believe in. As the company gets bigger, they become more like . . . well, coworkers. There's less warmth, less trust, and less time for and interest in building relationships.

Inflection Points and Complexity Bombs

The best leaders work hard to stay ahead of these problems, and they're often able to keep their organizations running pretty friction-free . . . until some inflection point occurs and suddenly they find themselves up to their ears in friction.

Growing companies want to keep growing—generally as fast as possible. To do that, they expand beyond their core: they launch new products, open new sales channels, and expand into new regions or countries. These expansion opportunities are analyzed in terms of their risk and return on investment before a decision is made. But even in well-run companies, leaders typically fail to assess their impact on organizational complexity. We saw that when OptiRoute opened their Memphis location.

SolAura only had one location—but it faced similar problems. SolAura is a direct-to-consumer business selling sun-care products based out of Miami. When I first met the team, they were generating meaningful sales and had seventy-five employees across six main departments: product development, supply chain, branding, online marketing, operations, and admin. All these departments were focused on the same goal, which was making the best possible sunscreen and selling as much of it as possible. Generally, their interactions were friction-free.

Once SolAura had established good traction in the D2C channel, Susannah, the CEO, decided they needed to be present in high-end physical retailers to help build the brand story. She created a new department to break into and manage that channel. But this department was different from the others—because now there were *two* departments responsible for selling product, and inevitably they had different ideas about how to position the brand, what pack sizes to sell, how to price them, and so on.

Soon there were numerous meetings in which the two different sales channels debated these points. Julio, the head of the D2C channel, didn't feel the need to consult with Alyssa, his counterpart from retail, on every decision—after all, his channel represented over 90 percent of the company's revenues. Alyssa found that she could never persuade Julio to go along with her ideas, so she gave up trying. Soon they were giving conflicting directions to the product development team—and then to the manufacturing teams—and it wasn't long until the company was mired in conflict.

Every time you add a new product, open a new region or channel, or expand into a new country, it unleashes a little Complexity Bomb. The reason is that you're creating the beginnings of a matrix organization.

If you've ever worked in a multinational company, you'll know what it means to work in a matrix organization—and that managing the matrix becomes a huge part of everyone's job. In a full-blown matrix, people frequently have three bosses: one linked to their region, one to their product or business unit, and one to their function. But when you have multiple bosses, no one boss can make a decision unless the others buy into it—otherwise you run into the SolAura problem.

That means that decisions can't be made over a coffee any longer—you'll need a slide deck and a socializing period. Meetings quickly multiply. Communication gets complicated, as information has to flow through multiple channels, and everyone wants it analyzed and presented differently. People end up spending more time on managing the decision-making process than they do on making the decision itself. Power struggles often break out as managers vie for control over shared resources and future direction.

Complexity Bombs occur every time you add an element to your business that introduces or expands some aspect of your organizational matrix. And that's when frictions really start to bite.

Hybrid and Remote Work Are Mini Bombs

Remote work unleashes another Complexity Bomb because it undermines the informal, spontaneous communications that created your Day Zero organization. Let's face it: a Zoom call is no substitute for a chat over a cup of coffee.

Working side by side with someone helps build trust. It's easier to work out disagreements when you can talk face-to-face. It's faster to coordinate things when you bump into your colleagues in the hallway. These small, unplanned moments are the reasons why Day Zero organizations are so friction-less. With remote or hybrid work, you miss out on this. Too many Zoom meetings, too many texts, and not enough effective conversations. You don't get to know your team the same way, and it's much harder to build a common culture.

Since COVID, I've worked with several founders whose organizations were partly or fully remote from the get-go, and every one of them has struggled to get the benefits of a Day Zero organization, even when they were very small.

Complexity Creates Friction, and Friction Slows You Down

When I started coaching CEOs of high-growth companies twelve years ago, I never imagined that organizational friction was going to become the focus of my work. As an ex-entrepreneur, I subscribed to the mantra that leaders should "get stuff done." I also shared the common belief that silos and other organizational dysfunctions were generally only big problems for large, mature organizations—but surely not for young, high-growth companies with entrepreneurial leaders.

I soon realized this wasn't true. I've come to think that organizational friction is a bit like arthritis—we think of it as a condition affecting older people, but sadly it affects young people (so-called early-onset arthritis) all too often. The organizational equivalent of early-onset arthritis is what I call the 3 Bs: *bureaucracy, bottlenecks,* and *bickering*—symptoms of an arthritic organization that you fully expect to encounter in a large enterprise but that turn up remarkably early in the life of high-growth companies. Because complexity grows exponentially, the 3 Bs take many leaders by surprise, causing them to wake up one day to find their organization is no long the fast-moving, nimble, and highly aligned unit it once was.

In fact, over the years, I've come to see that preventing and overcoming organizational friction is a bigger challenge for many CEOs than setting strategy, raising capital, or getting stuff done. The purpose of this book is to make sure that *you* are not taken by surprise—by equipping you with early detection systems, as well as the rituals that will enable your organization to stay high performing, agile, and flexible, even as you scale.

Recap

- Day Zero organizations, characterized by small highly aligned teams, typically perform well naturally.

- As your company grows, complexity grows exponentially. And complexity, unless carefully managed, creates frictions that will slow you down.

- Scaling means building an organization that performs better as it grows. It's not the same thing as growing, and the difference is mainly down to how well you manage friction.

- Leaders of high-growth companies naturally focus on the tangible drivers of growth—product improvement, marketing and sales, and securing funding. As a result, they're often the last people to know when organizational frictions develop.

- Blitzscaling (or hypergrowth) only works for a handful of companies. For many others, it results in an underperforming organization.

Chapter 2

What's a High-Performance Organization?

▼

This chapter will show you what a high-performing organization really looks like and how to define and measure that performance in a rigorous way. And you'll find out why the prevailing models of organizational performance don't really work.

I T'S HARD TO BE GREAT WHEN YOU DON'T KNOW what great looks like.

Before Roger Bannister became the first person to run a mile in under four minutes, everyone agreed the feat was physically impossible—some doctors even conjectured that the human body would explode at that speed. And if it were to be broken, track experts agreed that the conditions would have to be perfect: 68 degrees, no wind, running on hard, dry clay in front of a boisterous crowd urging the runner on.

But on May 6, 1954, Bannister came to the Iffley Road track in Oxford, England, to break the barrier. Conditions were far from ideal: the track was wet from a recent rain, a strong crosswind was blowing, and the crowd was small.

At 6 p.m., the starting gun was fired. For the first half mile, Bannister ran behind Chris Brasher, a former Cambridge runner who acted as his pacemaker. Then Chris Chataway took up the lead, and Bannister continued behind him. Finally, Bannister took the lead with about three hundred yards to go. He passed an unofficial timekeeper at the 1,500-meter mark in three minutes and forty-three seconds, equaling the world's record for that distance—and at that moment, Bannister threw in all his reserves, crossing the line with an exhausted yet triumphant smile. As soon as the first part of his score was announced—"three minutes"—the crowd erupted in pandemonium.

Runners had been attempting to break this barrier for at least a hundred years, and they had crept increasingly close over the twentieth century, yet the barrier remained unbroken, as much a psychological hurdle as a physical one. Yet only forty-six days later, John Landy broke the barrier, then four others did so within a year. A year later, three other runners ran a sub-four-minute mile in a single race, and since then, over 1,600 others have done the same.

What does that tell us?

Knowing what's possible and what to aim for changes everything in business as much as it does in sports. Founders and CEOs have plenty of clear benchmarks for assessing how their company is doing, such as winning an iconic customer, hitting their budget, raising funding from a top VC, becoming a unicorn, or reaching profitability.

But the metrics for assessing an organization are blurry. What's the four-minute mile of organizational performance?

In recent years, engagement surveys have become the main metric, and while these have certainly added some useful insights, they have important limitations. Apart from these simplistic surveys, most leaders don't know how to assess the performance of their organizations, so they focus on business results as the main proxy.

This has two problems. First, business results are a lagging indicator. The work your teams are doing now may not translate into measurable success or failure in the marketplace for many months, perhaps even years. You can't afford to wait that long to know whether your people, managers, teams, and cross-functional processes are operating at peak effectiveness or well below that. Second, it's a very poor proxy. Many factors, including those outside your control, will ultimately determine your company's performance: macroeconomic conditions, the state of the financial markets, changes in industry trends or regulation, and of course, what your competitors do.

That isn't to say that leaders have no idea how their teams or organizations are performing. While you may not be able to measure or define it, you probably know a high-performing organization when you see one. Unfortunately, that's not going to cut it if you're the person responsible for shaping and creating one, so we'll need to break it down to make sure you have an explicit understanding of what a high-performance organization is, how it's created, and how it's sustained as you scale.

Let's start by examining existing models of a high-performance organization. I've done an extensive literature review, and while there are many different philosophies and approaches, it turns out they nearly all boil down to one of two (opposing) visions—that high-performing organizations are either well-oiled machines or thriving communities.

High-Performing Organizations Are Well-Oiled Machines

Some thought leaders believe that to get your organization to high performance, you need to program it like a complex factory so that each part of the organization does exactly the right work at the right time, and all the individual units work together in unison. It's like one of those completely automated Japanese factories that make cars or vacuum cleaners, where each robot does its narrow job perfectly and operates in perfect harmony with the robots around it. There are no people involved, except perhaps when robots need to be maintained or repaired. In this world, management is judged purely by how many vacuum cleaners their factory churns out.

This is an analogy, but it's not far from the philosophy of many thought leaders on management. In their view, the definition of a high-performance organization is one that maximizes output. Everything should be as streamlined as possible. Like the robots in our Japanese factory, each production unit (i.e., person) should have clear roles and clear responsibilities. The output of their work should integrate perfectly with the output of the people working around them to create the final product that can be shipped to the next department or the external customer. Managers are there to design and orchestrate all these workflows, to measure the quality and output of the people they're responsible for, and from time to time, to tend to any "robots" that might need attention.

This philosophy was popularized by the legendary former CEO of Intel, Andy Grove, in his book *High Output Management*. Here's a quote: "The output of a manager is the output of the organizational units under his or her supervision or influence. . . . In principle every hour of your day should be spent increasing the output or the value of the output of the people whom you're responsible for." Many leaders embraced this worldview, including Jeff Bezos, Steve Jobs, Larry Ellison, and Steve Ballmer.

According to this philosophy, the key to high performance is to translate all the important outputs into easily measured terms—and to hold people accountable for these. That allows everyone to know what progress is being made and to drive further progress. So, it makes sense that Andy Grove invented OKRs (based on earlier work by Peter Drucker), and together with the VC John Doerr (who worked for Andy at Intel in the 1970s), helped popularize them.

This philosophy is simple, logical, and appealing. It does, however, have a flaw. In most modern companies, there are no robots. The people doing the "manufacturing" are, well, *people*. And people aren't machines. They need more than just an occasional visit from a maintenance man to remain motivated, perform at their best, and develop. And, unlike robots, people can quit.

(Ironically, tech companies are among the least automated companies you can find. Traditional businesses, such as steel mills, oil refineries, or indeed, vacuum manufacturers, employ a lot of process automation and are somewhat better suited to this approach. But if you think about the "manufacturing floor" of Google, Amazon, or any other tech company, all you'll see is people working on their laptops.)

High-Performing Organizations Are Thriving Communities

The second group of thought leaders take almost the opposite view: they see organizations as communities of people. For them, the signs of a healthy organization are when every member is inspired by a common purpose, impassioned by the mission, and connected through shared values. How people feel about their company and each other is front and center, and the presumption is that if the right feelings and relationships are in place, then the efficient production of vacuum cleaners will follow. In this worldview, psychological safety and diversity and inclusion take the place of efficiency and productivity as the core mantras.

Simon Sinek is perhaps the best-known proponent of this school of thought. In his book *Start with Why,* he writes: "People don't buy WHAT you do, they buy WHY you do it."

I can't see Andy Grove agreeing that people bought Intel's processors because of the company's *why*. In fact, I'm pretty sure he would say they bought them precisely because of their *what*—what their processors could do.

Simon also has a very different way of thinking about the role of managers and teams: "A team is not a group of people who work together. A team is a group of people who trust each other. . . . The role of a leader is not to come up with all the great ideas. It's to create an environment in which great ideas can happen . . . Leadership is not about being in charge. It's about taking care of those in your charge."[2] No mention of outputs here . . . or even of what work needs to be done, how it will be done, or by whom. In this worldview, it's the culture, not the programming of work, that is key to performance. And proponents of this worldview would argue that culture attracts the best talent—after all, why would the top talent want to work in a company that treats them like a cog in a machine? (To which the first group would respond: because they love to get stuff done and are paid very well to do it.)

Examples of successful companies that have tilted toward this worldview include LinkedIn, Zappos under Tony Hsieh's

---

[2] This comes from one of Simon Sinek's LinkedIn posts. See it here: linkedin.com/posts/ simonsinek_a-team-is-not-a-group-of-people-who-work-activity-6780192942679179264-pYtP.

leadership, Pixar, Patagonia, and Southwest Airlines.

So, which is it? Are organizations machines that need to be programmed or communities that need to be nurtured? As a CEO, should you be the master programmer: data driven, analytical, and objective? Or should you be the ultimate team builder: values driven, inclusive, and supportive?

If you start to search for insights on how to build a high-performance organization in your company, you'll soon see that nearly every management guru falls distinctly into one camp or the other. The problem is . . . they're both right.

Forging an Integrated Approach

It's not hard to find companies that have been successful following one or the other of these models. Machine-oriented companies like Amazon value productivity above all else and drive toward it relentlessly at every level—sometimes to the point of driving talented people away. But it works for them—because they can draw on a global talent pool and pay top dollar for "super athletes" who thrive in this atmosphere. Can you?

Community-oriented companies like LinkedIn and Zappos place a huge focus on building strong teams, shared values, and happy employees, but they aren't always so great at maximizing productivity. It works for them because their core businesses are so profitable that they don't need to squeeze every ounce of productivity out of their people (or, as in the case of Patagonia, because their owners aren't very concerned with profitability). Can you say the same for yours?

The unavoidable truth is that you need both. You need ambitious goals, systems to translate those goals into well-organized workstreams, and metrics to track your progress against them. You need your people to deliver. But to get that, you also need a shared vision, great leadership, high trust, and a culture that attracts great talent, brings out the best in your people, and encourages seamless collaboration.

If I translate that into high-level outcomes, I'd define a high-performance organization as one that delivers great results for customers, investors, and employees—all three or it's not truly high-performance.

However, as we saw earlier, creating value for these three stakeholders is a long-term process, so we'll need a way of tracking how our organizations are performing day-to-day—a way to translate these high-level outcomes into metrics that apply at a granular level and that are leading rather than lagging indicators.

Productivity and Positivity

Over the years, I've experimented with different approaches and have settled on two simple measures that work extremely well. I call them Productivity and Positivity.

Productivity is reasonably straightforward: it's not just about how much work is being done per unit of time or per person. It's about getting the *right* work done—the work that will ultimately create value for customers and shareholders—and doing that work in a reasonably efficient way. We'll talk much more about Productivity later, but because it's quite intuitive, let's turn our focus to the other side.

Positivity sounds nice, but what does it mean? Most leaders can come up with a definition, but it's typically not a definition that gets us where we need to be. Too often, this side of the equation has been viewed through the superficial lens of *making people happy to be at work*. This understanding of Positivity leads executives to offer what are effectively perks, like free lunches, stylish offices, staff parties, game rooms, luxury bus rides to the office, or increasingly, the option for employees to do their work from the comfort of their living rooms.

There's nothing intrinsically wrong with these things—apart from the obvious fact that they all take either time or money, both of which are inherently scarce resources. From this frame, the more one invests in Positivity, the less time and money are available to invest in Productivity. And while free lunches, fancy offices, or the occasional party *might* lead to increased Productivity, it's awfully hard to know for sure—and most leaders are legitimately skeptical.

A Shift in Perspective

The key to unlocking a world in which your organization can be *both* highly Productive and highly Positive, and not have these be in tension with each other, is to shift the way you think about Positivity: from focusing on making your people happy *to come to work*, to making them happy *doing the work*.

Positivity is about running your company so that people feel great about their experience of doing the work itself—whether they are programmers or senior executives. And nothing determines how people feel about their work more than the quality of the interactions they have with their colleagues. We'll get into this in much more detail soon.

Sustainable performance is the sweet spot where Productivity and Positivity are both high—where your team achieves great things *and* feels good about their lived experience as they achieve them.

> The key to unlocking a world in which your organization can be *both* highly Productive and highly Positive, and not have these be in tension with each other, is to shift the way you think about Positivity: from focusing on making your people happy *to come to work*, to making them happy *doing the work*.

Don't Be a Flip-Flopper

Day Zero organizations often start with high Productivity and Positivity, but because the Positivity happens naturally, leaders focus mostly on the Productivity side. They understand the need for Positivity as well, but because they have the wrong definition of Positivity—one in which it's a scarce resource—they end up becoming flip-floppers. In other words, they only focus on Positivity when things are going well and they have a bit of spare time or money. Now is the time to introduce a superficial feel-good factor, like holding an all-staff party, giving out new company swag, or offering training. Even worse, some executives wait until their employee engagement scores hit rock bottom—and then reach for these simplistic quick fixes to address the "engagement problem."

But precisely because their approach to Positivity is too superficial to make any real difference, they soon get frustrated with the lack of results and revert to focusing on Productivity.

Why do so many executives end up taking the flip-flopping approach? Because *they see Productivity and Positivity as being in tension with each other*—which means the more time they spend on one side, the less they have for the other. That mindset is doomed to fail. It's also wrong because it's based on the faulty definition of Positivity we saw earlier.

They see Productivity and Positivity as being in tension with each other—which means the more time they spend on one side, the less they have for the other. That mindset is doomed to fail.

If you think of Positivity as upgrading the office decor, offering free food, or throwing an office party, then the tension *is* real—because these things take time and money but don't improve Productivity.

But once you recognize that Positivity is not about "making people happy to come to work" but is about "making people happy with their experience of doing the work," then this tension melts away. Now you and your fellow leaders can be *driving both at the same time, all the time.*

But it gets better. Because, as we will soon see, the form of Positivity I'm talking about has a direct link to Productivity, and vice versa. When viewed correctly, they support each other. Now we're no longer in a world where Productivity and Positivity are in tension—or even independent of each other—but are in a mutually reinforcing virtuous circle.

Interactions Are the Foundation

Earlier we defined a high-performance organization as one that generates good outcomes for all key stakeholders, including customers, investors, and employees. We saw the need to translate these high-level objectives into a more immediate frame of reference, which brought us to Productivity and Positivity. But how can you measure those in a way that allows you to wire them into the daily life of your organization?

The key is to focus on a particular aspect of work that underpins them both. That unit is human interactions.

It's easy to see how interactions can impact Positivity. If someone ignores us, or criticizes our project, or we hear through the grapevine that they don't think highly of us, that's not going to make us feel great.

By contrast, it's tempting to think of Productivity as something individuals achieve on their own: how fast they crunch their data, generate new marketing materials, or execute their sales calls. These may be good measures of their *activity* level, but the factor determining how much value their activity creates is the quality of the interactions that preceded this activity. So, let's look at how ordinary interactions can impact both Productivity and Positivity.

A Bad Day at the Office

HyperDrive is a fast-growing SaaS company with a performance-oriented culture, very much spearheaded by their founder and CEO, Adyen. Adyen's motto is "Always be shipping, and always be selling." With the intense pace that he sets, everyone works incredibly hard, but communications aren't always as effective as they could be, or decisions as carefully made. Here is a snapshot of three situations at HyperDrive that I encountered.

Tracey is a senior data analyst in the data science department. She loves her job and thrives on the high-intensity, deadline-driven atmosphere. She'd spent a week crunching data for a new product feature and sent her findings to the product team. A chat notification popped up from Didi, the product manager, asking her to call.

Didi: Tracey, the way you've presented this data is great, but last week we adjusted the product slightly, so you'll need to adjust your analysis a little. Is that okay?

Tracey: When did you decide this, and why didn't I know?

Didi: Adam and I agreed to it on a call. I didn't know we were going to be talking about this, or I would have included you. And then afterward I just go so busy that I forgot to tell you until now.

Tracey: Okay, but I really wish I'd known sooner. We need to loop in data science earlier to avoid this kind of rework. Anyway, I'll get it done."

A sinking feeling came over her. Although the product

team wouldn't be aware of it, she knew that she would have to redo much of the work. At least a week's worth of work was basically wasted.

Nikhil had recently been hired by the marketing department to produce B2B marketing collateral. His background was in B2C marketing, which had been raised as a concern by the recruiter, but Josef, his hiring manager, was in a hurry to build up his team and decided that it would be fine.

But Nikhil was finding that his work was frequently shot down. He had started to doubt himself and lose motivation. Later in the afternoon, another downer of an email came in from Josef: "Nikhil, this material isn't going to resonate with our clients. It's too simplistic and not technical enough. Can you rework this?"

Trying to manage his emotions, he responded: "Thanks, Josef, for the feedback. I'm committed to improving, but I feel I'm flying a little blind here. I could really use a little more guidance or training so that I can deliver better results."

Josef replied: "I hear you. I'd love to get that for you, just not sure when we'll be able to get to it, but know that I've got your back. In the meantime, please redo this as per my earlier feedback."

Carolyn is a high-performing salesperson, but she's had a rough quarter. James, her boss, had recently reorganized the account coverage plan, moving from an industry to a regional model. She expressed her concerns at the time, but he didn't seem to take them seriously and went ahead with his original plan. Now she's working with a bunch of companies in industries she doesn't really understand, performing poorly, and feeling discouraged as a result. Then came the call: "Carolyn, your numbers are not looking good this quarter. What's going on? What's your plan?"

Visibly upset, she responded: "James, I mentioned my concerns about the reorganization. You've got me managing clients in industries I'm not familiar with. I'm doing my best, and I'm sure I'll get there, but it's not going to happen overnight."

James said, "Okay, but the pressure is coming straight from the top, so we really do need to hit our numbers this quarter. I'd be happy to carry you this quarter if I had a buffer from some other sector, but I don't. You'll just have to do your best."

Carolyn: "Understood."

In all these examples, poor upstream interactions had a significant impact on the Productivity of a talented, motivated person down the road. They also undermined Positivity by making their work a frustrating, anxiety-inducing, or discouraging experience instead of a rewarding one. Of course, I have chosen particularly stark examples to illustrate the point, and it's not always as direct or impactful, but my goal is simply to help you see the link between human interactions, Productivity, and Positivity.

We saw earlier how the number of interactions between people grows exponentially as your head count grows. Putting these ideas together, we start to see the nature of the challenge: we need a way to ensure that the daily interactions taking place across your organization are supporting both Productivity and Positivity, even as the number of potential interactions grows exponentially.

A Great Day at the Office

Unlike his less fortunate colleagues, Jim, the VP of operations, was feeling super excited about his work at HyperDrive. When I shadowed him for a day, it soon became clear why.

His day kicked off with a meeting on his most important

project. It soon became clear that his boss, Lucas, the COO, had great communication and meeting management skills. Over the next forty-five minutes, the four people in the meeting ran through the key challenges on Jim's project. They resolved several issues on the spot and agreed to come back to one big challenge after they'd done more investigation. A time and date were set for the follow-up. Toward the end, everyone shared a brief update on what they'd be focusing on in the coming week and where they might need help or input from someone else on the call.

The energy on the call was great—there was plenty of debate but also moments of calm where people really listened to each other and thought about the best approach. Everyone contributed their thoughts, and their ideas seemed to build on each other. What struck me most is how they resolved one of their challenges—instead of just debating the two approaches that various team members had put forward, Lucas led a conversation that helped the team come up with a new approach, which they kept refining until everyone was happy with it. Finally, Lucas closed the meeting by expressing his appreciation for the good teamwork, and everyone left in high spirits. The meeting was the tangible expression of high Productivity and Positivity.

I continued to shadow Jim through the rest of his day, sitting in on a few short one-to-ones and a longer meeting with his own direct reports. He'd clearly picked up some skills from Lucas, as all his conversations were as constructive and energizing as the call led by Lucas. He walked out of the office at 7 p.m. with a spring in his step.

Can you remember the last time you had a day like that? And how that day made you feel? Excited, energized, on a roll. Happy to be working with that team. On days like this, you're eager to get home and tell your partner what a great day you've had at work.

Also, imagine that you had days like this all the time. When days like this become the norm, you go home and tell your partner how much you love your job.

Now, imagine that everyone in your company had days like this all the time. When your people consistently experience these kinds of great interactions, you won't need to offer free lunches or massages. Employees will give their very best *and* tell their friends what a great place it is to work. Now the pursuit of Productivity and Positivity are not in tension but in harmony. No flip-flopping, no internal inconsistencies.

That's a high-performance organization.

But how do we get there?

Recap

- Leaders have clear ways of assessing their companies' performance in terms of revenues, profits, or customer metrics, but assessing the performance of their organization is more challenging.

- Business results are a poor proxy for the health of your organization in the short term.

- Some leaders see high-performing organizations as well-oiled machines with streamlined processes and clear roles and responsibilities; others see them as thriving communities with a shared purpose and values and a cohesive culture. Both perspectives have their merits, and successful companies reflecting both paradigms can be found.

- Sustainable high performance requires integrating these two philosophies. Thinking in terms of Productivity and Positivity helps, but most people misunderstand Positivity.

- The key to reconciling these two approaches is to shift the definition of Positivity from making people happy to *come* to work to making them happy with their experience of *doing* the work.

- People's experience of work is largely driven by the quality of their human interactions

- Many leaders fall into the trap of flip-flopping between focusing on Productivity and then on Positivity, but this approach is flawed. Sustainable performance occurs when leaders recognize that true Positivity and Productivity are not in tension but are mutually reinforcing.

Chapter 3

Dialogue Is Your Operating System

▼

In this chapter, you will learn how the quality of your conversations determines the results you achieve in your business—and how dialogue can be the upgraded operating system for your company.

IMAGINE AN EXPERIMENT WITH TWO TEAMS meeting in separate rooms. The rooms have one-way mirrors so you can see the people inside, but they can't see you. You can hear them well enough to get the tone and meeting dynamics, but you can't quite make out all the words. If I tell you that one team is high performing and the other isn't, do you think you can tell which is which?

Of course you can. In the high-performing team, everyone is engaged and contributing. They're making eye contact with each other, and no one is looking at their phone. When one person speaks, everyone else listens—and there don't seem to be a lot of interruptions. You hear people asking questions, not just making statements. You can feel how people are working together, building on each other's thoughts. What don't you see? All the behaviors that make meetings uncomfortable and ineffective, like interrupting, tuning out, holding back, defending, dominating, and dismissing.

Now imagine you're observing one-to-one conversations between managers and their direct reports in the same way. Can you tell who is the better manager? Once again, you can. In one room, both parties look relaxed, engaged, and open. Both are contributing to the conversation. There's no sense of anxiety or fear. In the other, the manager is doing all the talking, and the subordinate looks anxious—and you sense he's on the defensive when he speaks. In one case, the subordinate emerges motivated and clear on what to do. In the other case, frustrated and dejected.

Anytime two or more people in your organization interact, the impact of their interaction on both Productivity and Positivity is obvious: if you could observe them like in the experiment above, you'd see it, hear it, and feel it.

And if you're a participant in the meeting, your body intuitively registers how things are going: If you're sitting through a long set of updates and no real progress is being made, you'll get squirmy and impatient. If people are talking past each other and not recognizing what their misunderstanding is about, you'll sense your frustration rising. And if people are interrupting, attacking, dismissing, or undermining others, you'll feel a palpable sense of discomfort in your gut and spine.

But when a meeting is going spectacularly well, with everyone jumping in to contribute, new ideas popping up, people listening and building on each other's thoughts, and real progress being made on important issues, your body will be vibrating with positive energy.

Great interactions like this drive both Productivity and Positivity, the key ingredients of sustainable high performance. In this chapter, you'll learn how effective dialogue is the underpinning of all these different interactions—in fact, how it can be the new operating system that drives your company's ability to scale smoothly.

What Is Your Company Made Of?

Let me ask you a philosophical question: What is your company made of? Is it made of money? Well, of course it took money to create the company, but if that's all it took, then all companies would look identical.

Is it made of people? Yes—but without them interacting and, having conversations, then all those people would just be standing around, not knowing what to do.

Is it made of ideas? Most certainly, but how many people had great ideas that never led to anything? And did those ideas organize themselves into the products and services you have today?

No, the thing that best captures what your company is built on is one word: *conversations*. If you are a founder, it started with the conversations you had with your cofounders, prospective customers, early investors, and first hires. If you're a leader in a larger company, it's the conversations you—and hundreds of colleagues before you—had that resulted in today's product offerings, customers, and capabilities. Indeed, if you had a magic microscope that could peer into the origins of everything your company does—every product, every marketing strategy, and every line of code in your business—you'd see that they were all the result of the conversations that preceded them.

Your company is built on one word:
conversations.

The quality of the conversations we have largely determines the quality of the products, strategies, business processes, and hiring decisions that result from them. But not all conversations are equally good or produce equally good results. The best conversations are those where people *think together* to harness the collective intelligence, knowledge, insights, and experience of the people involved. And that is what I call dialogue.

Dialogue is not a very charming word. It sounds dry and technical—I much prefer the word *conversation*. But I need to keep the word in play here to make a clear distinction between a high-quality dialogue and a typical, casual conversation.

Both involve speaking and listening, but dialogue has one more crucial element: thinking. In fact, the original meaning of the word in ancient Greek was "a flow of meaning." For there to be a flow of meaning, we need to go beyond just talking together. We need to learn from each other. And once we have learned something from each other, we need to think together. In short, dialogue is the act of learning and thinking together, or to keep it simple, the act of *collective thinking*.

Why is the kind of dialogue that generates collective thinking so important?

Ordinary conversations are great for all kinds of things— deciding where to have lunch, organizing an event, or updating people on the status of your project. But when there's an important matter at hand, and people hold strong views about it, then ordinary conversations don't have a great track record.

Everyone Has a Different Perspective

There are two fundamentally different types of conversations—"it" and "us"—and each carries its own intrinsic challenge. "It" conversations are all about your business: strategy, targets, customers, projects, products, money. "Us" conversations are about, well, us: how we are getting along or working together, who is better suited to taking on a particular role, what went wrong in the team meeting that caused someone to walk out upset. We'll return to the challenges of "us" conversations in chapter 6.

People are generally comfortable dealing with "it" issues . . . until there's some meaningful disagreement. How often have you gone into a discussion thinking, "This one's a no-brainer— the answer is clear as day," only to find that, lo and behold, other people see it quite differently? Maybe they don't agree on the problem. Or they agree on the problem but not on the solution. Or perhaps they even agree on the solution—but for completely different reasons. The reality is that everyone has their own unique perspective on almost everything.

If by some strange chance you went to a meeting where everyone saw the issues the same way, the meeting would be fun—you could all congratulate and high-five each other on how smart you are—but *it would also be a complete waste of time.*

This points to a simple but profound truth: the purpose of any meeting that can add real value is to explore different perspectives in order to *generate ideas, solutions, and decisions that are better than any one person could have come up with on their own.* After all, if we're not coming up with something over the course of a meeting that is better than we started with—why have it at all?

This is the essence of collective thinking. The problem is that it happens all too rarely.

The Right/Wrong Frame

Take a moment to consider the interactions in your company. Do you see people exhibiting any of these behaviors?

- **Pushing their ideas but not listening to others**

- Dominating conversations, making it difficult for others to get a word in

- Discounting the views of others

- Using power or position to force an outcome

- Making light of others' concerns

- Going along with a decision that they don't really believe in to avoid conflict

In most organizations, these things happen all the time. In fact, many of us are so accustomed to these behaviors that we have stopped noticing how harmful and destructive they are. Instead, we just push through until the issue at hand is resolved one way or the other, and then we move on—rather than trying to improve the underlying interaction that went wrong in the first place.

These behaviors are all reflections of a frame of mind in which one idea (mine!) is (entirely) right—and other ideas (all of yours!) are therefore (entirely) wrong. In this world, there are only winners and losers. Even in situations where you may not see these unhelpful behaviors, the right/wrong, win/ lose mentality still tends to prevail—and it prevents collective thinking.

We see this in the many conversations that debate existing ideas ("Should we go with Nick's idea, or Susan's?") but fail to explore and develop new ideas—ideas that might reflect knowledge and insights of people other than Nick or Susan. Such debates often descend into unproductive ping-pong matches where people try to prove they're right rather than explore potential solutions that are better than the existing options. These discussions typically result in a preening winner, a frustrated loser, and a lack of real commitment.

Reframing

A simple but powerful reframe will help you navigate differences in perspective and generate collective thinking much more successfully. If we can replace our right/wrong frame with the starting assumption that we're probably both *partly right*, then this naturally leads to very different behaviors.

If we can replace our right/wrong frame with the starting assumption that we're probably both *partly right*, then this naturally leads to very different behaviors.

This assumption is the essence of intellectual humility. If we're both super confident in our point of view, then we will inevitably approach any disagreement with a win/lose frame of mind. But if we're both aware that our insights and knowledge have limits, that we can never have all the relevant information, that others may have information or insights that we lack, *and that even we can make mistakes*, then we will naturally approach these types of conversations very differently. In this world, we naturally assume we have something to learn from each other, and that changes everything.

Once we have each learned from the other—shared the information I had that you didn't, explained the option you could see that I couldn't, explored the constraints that you were aware of that I was not—then we are heading in the right direction. Collective thinking enables us to explore what's most compelling and relevant in different people's thinking—as well as what is not so robust—so that we can build something better than what we started with.

When there are only two people in a discussion, it's not so hard to achieve this synergy, but it becomes dramatically harder as the number of people in the room grows. In larger meetings, a small minority typically dominate the airtime, leaving others struggling to get a word in edgewise—or, more often, not even bothering to try. By the time you have ten people or more, it's really challenging to harness the collective intelligence of the room and not spend all day doing it. And this is, of course, all much more difficult when meetings are virtual.

So that's why we need to master the art of collective thinking, both for groups of two and for larger groups. Because when people are truly thinking and learning together, then new, better solutions emerge that harness the diversity in your organization by drawing on the knowledge and insights of everyone involved. People experience these conversations as powerful, energizing, and time incredibly well spent. They are the embodiment of Productivity.

And when each person involved in that conversation feels that their voice was heard and that they had at least some influence on the outcome, then they will feel far more committed to taking the plan forward—as well as to giving their very best to this group the next time it works together. That is the embodiment of Positivity. (It's also a very good working definition of inclusivity.)

Later, we will get into how we can practice collective thinking in larger groups, but first let's master a core skill—and our first ritual—that will ground our collective thinking skills in any size group.

The Ladder of Inference

The key tool that helps us learn from each other so that we can generate collective thinking is the ladder of inference. Developed by Professor Chris Argyris of the Harvard Business School, it's a model that explains how we reach our conclusions.[3]

---

[3] For more information, see pon.harvard.edu/daily/negotiation-skills-daily/the-ladder-of-inference-a-resource-list.

Here's how it works.

There's a vast amount of information out there on any given topic. We can never have access to all of it—but we often assume the information we do have access to is all that we need. From there, we start to select the information (often subconsciously) we find most compelling. Then we try to make sense of it: We analyze it. We draw some initial conclusions. We refine those further based on our beliefs about what's most important. From there we draw our conclusions.

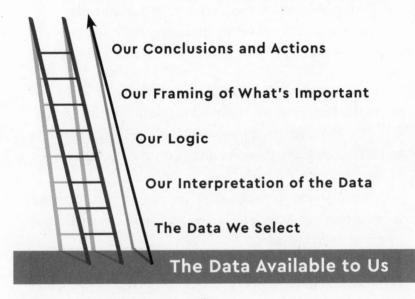

Figure 3.1. The ladder of inference.

The most common reason why "it" conversations go so wrong is because people often stay "too high" on their ladder. Instead of explaining the thought process that led to their conclusion, and the information they based that thought process on, they simply present their conclusion as if it's obvious. This often sounds innocuous enough in phrases such as "Clearly, the best way forward is . . ." or "It's obvious that we have to . . ." And the more competition there is in the room to be right, the more likely this behavior is.

But what is "obviously" right to you may be obviously wrong to me. When people present their views in this way, they set the stage for a win/lose battle. In response, we naturally respond from the top of *our* ladder: "That will never work." "You don't understand the situation." Soon, the frictions build.

But what is "obviously" right to you may be obviously wrong to me. When people present their views in this way, they set the stage for a win/lose battle.

You're probably not aware of it when you start at the top of your ladder. After all, we're all prone to jumping to conclusions. The more expert you are on a topic, the easier it is to make such leaps unconsciously. But to keep these types of conversations from reaching an impasse, you'll need to understand where your colleagues are coming from and make it easier for them to understand where you're coming from— by going down the ladder.

By sharing and comparing our ladders, we can find the point at which our thinking diverges. Maybe I have information that you don't. Maybe you think I'm ignoring something that's vitally important. Maybe I can point out how your interpretation of the data is flawed. These are specific steps that you can test and resolve—whereas before, all you had were two irreconcilable conclusions. In short, the ladder helps us harness our collective intelligence and come up with solutions that are better than either one of us could have produced alone. This is constructive conflict at its best.

Ritual 1:
Thinking Together

The ladder of inference is a wonderful model and a powerful tool, and this ritual presents the simplest possible way to put it into use: asking questions. This makes it easy to have consistently Productive and Positive "it" discussions even when you and your discussion partners have very different perspectives.

Step 1: Get set up. Make sure you know what you're there to discuss. Are you trying to decide between two options? Or diagnose what's going wrong in a part of your business?

Step 2: Ask and listen. Ask your colleague what their thinking is on the issue at hand, and settle in to listen deeply and fully. Breathe. If you're in the same room or on a videoconference call, keep your eyes on them so they know you're really listening. Relax your face and jaw. Use your body language and verbal cues (e.g., mm-hmm) to signal that you're interested in what they have to say and that they should take all the time they need to finish their thoughts. *Under no circumstances should you interrupt.*

Step 3: Ask what else. When they've finished their initial train of thought, don't jump in—not yet. Patience is the key to this ritual. Instead, ask them to keep going—what else do they think? What else do they want you to understand? Settle back in and listen more, with the same undivided attention. By the time they finish, chances are excellent that they'll have revealed most of their ladder (without them even having to know what the ladder is).

Step 4: Ask deepening questions. If you agree with everything they've said so far, then your meeting is effectively over—you can high-five and move on! If not, resist the usual temptation to counter with your thinking. Instead, it's time to ask deepening questions. These are questions designed to help you understand their ladder more deeply. The question you choose will reflect where on their ladder you feel you may be seeing things differently. There are an infinite number of such questions, but here are a few great ones:

- What data or information was most influential in shaping your thinking?

- What alternative solutions did you consider, and why did you reject them?

- Can you illustrate your thinking with an example?

- What problem were you trying to solve? (This is a great one if you really can't connect with their thinking at all—perhaps they're actually trying to solve a different problem than the one you thought you were discussing.)

- What's the single most important thing I need to understand?

As they answer your questions, just listen. Look for points of agreement as well as differences, and as always, *don't interrupt.*

Step 5: Paraphrase. Ask them, "Can I replay what you're saying and you let me know if I've properly understood it?"

Step 6: Share your perspective. Now it's your turn. If this topic is important to you and you're like most human beings, you have no doubt been impatient to say what *you* think. This is natural: we're all eager to express our opinions, and it can be hard to listen as long as you have without sharing your views. But trust that the time you have spent listening will pay off handsomely now for three reasons: (1) you fully understand their thinking, (2) you know where on the ladder your thinking diverges from theirs, so you can start there rather than making points that aren't central to your disagreement, and (3) because your colleague feels completely heard by you, they should be more relaxed and ready to truly listen to you. (And, as an added benefit, you're role-modeling a supremely constructive behavior that will serve your entire company well as it scales.) As you explain your thinking, make it easy for your colleague to understand where you're coming from by using the ladder. Share the information you're relying on, make your logic explicit, and indicate that you're open to all of it being questioned, tested, or challenged.

Step 7: Search for a joint solution. Start with any common ground and work forward together from there. Remember that the goal is to come up with something that reflects the best of all of your thinking. Of course, there may still be points on which you disagree—there's no magic cure for that—but the hundreds of clients who have used this ritual report that it has helped them build a common view dramatically faster and with far fewer frustrations. Following this pattern of conversation will help:

- Share *one* thought at a time. It might take fifteen seconds or a minute, but don't string lots of thoughts together— that makes it too hard for the other person to both fully absorb your thinking and consider their response.

- When your thought is done, signal that you're done and that you're interested in their perspective by asking your colleague, "What do you think?"

- Now maintain the same quality of attention as before: look curious, keep your eyes on your colleague, and don't interrupt.

- Take turns like this. Respect the quality of each other's time.

When you're finished, you should notice that this approach not only leads to ideas, solutions, and decisions that are better than those you had at the start—*but also that feels like you're building on each other's thoughts.* This makes conversations feel both highly Productive and Positive.

At one level, this is just the age-old wisdom of seeking to understand before making yourself understood. But this goes deeper than traditional active listening. Done properly, you'll find that you are actually able to affect the quality, depth, and clarity of your partners' thinking simply through the quality of your listening and attention. Soon, their underlying concern, the one piece of information their argument hinges on, or the consideration that is so important to them, shines through clearly, stripped of all the extraneous argumentation they might have felt the need for in a more competitive or combative environment.

This is the most foundational of all the rituals—if you aren't able to ask good questions, and then shut up and listen without interrupting when you need to, nothing else you learn in this book is going to work.

As simple as this ritual is—essentially just asking questions and listening—like any new habit, you may need a reminder at first. For a year I carried around a list of deepening questions printed out on a business card. At the start of important meetings, I would place it next to my pad of paper as a gentle reminder. All it takes is a few weeks of conscious practice, and soon you and your team will be doing this automatically.

The Thinking Together Ritual might feel a bit slow or awkward at first, but before you give up on it, imagine the following possible future. Your company has grown to hundreds or thousands of employees—yet this way of handling differing perspectives has become the norm across your organization. Everywhere you go, in different offices, business units, and countries, you see people asking great questions, listening deeply, taking time to understand other people's points of view, and challenging thinking in a fact-and-logic-driven way—rather than doing combat at the tops of their ladders.

Are you sure you want to walk away from that future?

Measuring Dialogue

Companies measure revenues, costs, and profits. Actually, they measure hundreds if not thousands of things, and this makes sense—how would you know if your inventory levels needed to be adjusted, or your sales funnel refined, if you didn't measure them?

So, it's strange that we don't measure the one thing that preceded and shaped all these outcomes, which is the quality of the conversations that led to them (and the meetings in which these conversations take place). If you add up all the time that people in your organization spend in meetings and multiply by their salaries, I think you'll find that *meetings are the single biggest expenditure you don't track.* So, we're neither measuring the cost of these meetings nor their quality and effectiveness.

But the good news is that the quality of your dialogue is easily measurable, so let's dive in.

Productivity

What makes for a Productive dialogue depends, of course, on the purpose and the topic of the conversation: brainstorming is different from problem-solving is different from coordinating execution plans. Yet we all know in our gut whether a conversation has been Productive. Think about the last five meetings you participated in and ask yourself how valuable they were. I'm confident you'll have a clear gut-level answer—even if the nature of these meetings was different.

It took me some time to reverse engineer this built-in gut indicator we all have, and here is the result:

- Did we work on an important issue? (Because even a great conversation isn't that Productive if we're talking about where to hold the company picnic.)

- Did we have a clear purpose for the discussion? (Because setting an explicit purpose helps us guide the meeting to achieve it.)

- Did we harness the collective intelligence of the group to generate ideas and decisions that were better than what we could have done alone? (Because collective thinking leads to better outcomes.)

- Did we build a shared commitment to a clear course of action? (Because clarity and commitment lead to effective execution.)

- Did we make good progress relative to the time spent? (Because time matters.)

A simple way to think about Productivity is to ask yourself the question, "How did we do?" If you feel the two of you—or the ten of you—did a great job of addressing whatever the issue at hand was, and didn't take longer than needed, then that's probably a Productive dialogue.

Positivity

Positivity can be even more confusing. Often clients mistake this for being polite or being gentle with each other (i.e., avoiding open disagreements or tiptoeing around awkward issues). This is definitively *not* what I'm talking about. It's perfectly possible—in fact, quite necessary—for you to be able to disagree, debate, and challenge each other. It's also necessary—and possible—to be able to have awkward and even sensitive discussions that are still Positive.

Here are the best questions to ask to assess the Positivity of your conversations and meetings:

- Was everyone paying full attention? (Because if people are texting or multitasking in other ways, it's disrespectful and disheartening to the others.)

- Did everyone feel psychologically safe? (Because if anyone felt censored, criticized, undermined, or attacked, that's obviously not going to be a great experience for them.)

- Did everyone get a chance to contribute their best thinking? (Because if a minority dominate the conversation, leaving others feeling they were unable to contribute, that's demotivating.)

- Did everyone feel that their views were given genuine consideration? (Because if someone senses their views are being ignored, or that others aren't keeping an open mind, that's frustrating—and at odds with the principles of collective thinking.)

Where Productivity is a group-level measurement, Positivity is very much down to the individual. The simplest way to think about it is to ask yourself the question, "How did I feel?" If you felt happy with the way you and others were treated, and the others did too, then that's a Positive conversation. And if you managed to feel that way while having have some tough discussions or debates, then that's going to lead to a surge in trust for the people in the room, as you'll learn in chapter 6.

I encourage my clients to use a simple 2x2 that I call the Productivity and Positivity matrix, as shown in figure 3.2, to measure the quality of their dialogue. This simple framework works equally well for one-to-ones between a manager and subordinate as for an executive committee or board. Later, in the Coach Your Team from the Balcony Ritual (page 149), we'll learn how you can use this to coach your own teams, but for now let's just use it as a simple measurement tool.

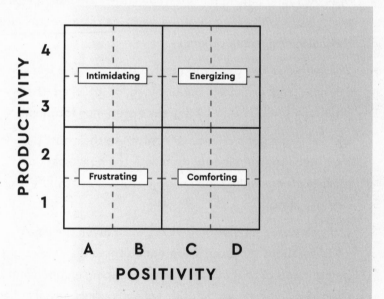

Figure 3.2. The Productivity and Positivity matrix.

I mentioned earlier that we all have a great internal meter for sensing how Productive a conversation or meeting is. It shouldn't come as a surprise, then, that we have an even better meter for sensing Positivity, since it's very much a subjective measure of our own experience. So, the next time you're in a meeting, ask yourself, "Which quadrant of the 2x2 are we in?" You can literally feel it in your body.

If you're in the Frustrating quadrant—where nothing useful is being accomplished *and* you're not feeling great about how you (or others) are being treated—then you'll almost certainly feel restless, agitated, distracted, and a little annoyed. In this state, it's very tempting to pull out your phone and start doing something else!

If you're in the Comforting quadrant—where the conversation is friendly, pleasant, and not entirely unproductive, but not Productive enough to fully energize you—you'll probably feel relaxed, warm toward the others, but perhaps a little bored or uninspired. After a while, you'll want to wrap it up, as you have too many other important calls on your time.

If you're in the Intimidating quadrant—where you're dealing with important issues and making real headway but people's behaviors are less than fully comfortable for you—you'll probably feel engaged but also a little tense, agitated, or on edge.

And when you're in the Energizing quadrant—where you and your colleagues are getting plenty of important work done and you're loving the vibe—you're going to feel engaged, motivated, energized, and happy.

It's important to remember that what may feel Comforting to you may be Intimidating to others, and vice versa, so it's important to check in with everyone to see how they're experiencing the meeting.

Dialogue Beats Systems Hands Down

If you lean toward a Productivity-oriented view of the world, I can imagine that you might be rolling your eyes at all this talk about dialogue. From the "organization as a machine" perspective, it's clear goals, efficient processes, and data-driven management systems that help your company succeed and scale, not just a load of talk. While it's true that you'll need systems and processes to scale, let's examine what they can and cannot do for you.

Not long ago, one of my long-term clients faced a tough decision: either promote a senior department head to a general management position that he probably wasn't ready for or risk losing him. The employee had a strong competing offer, so the choice was pretty stark.

This company has an excellent chief people officer and a genuine commitment to developing its staff, so it also has a rigorous performance management process, including regular 360 reviews. When we sat down to discuss this case, I naturally asked to look at the employee's reviews. I gathered that he was good at his job and was improving over time. Based on that data alone, I would have supported his promotion with no reservations.

But I also decided to talk to a few of the people who worked most closely with him. Instead of seeking general feedback on his current performance, I asked them some specific questions about the skills he would need to be successful in the new role. Their answers gave me serious reservations about the promotion.

This was a powerful reminder of one limitation of business systems: they are only as good as the questions they were designed to answer. In fact, most systems can't "answer" much of anything—even the best systems are useless without human intervention. Your accounting system can tell you that your costs are over budget, but it can't tell you what to do about it. Your project management system can let you know which projects are behind schedule, but it can't tell you why or help you get them back on track. Your HR system can show that turnover is higher than last year, but it can't reverse the trend.

These limits are fine as soon as we realize that, in fact, all management systems exist for just one purpose: *to spark and inform human dialogue.*

Ultimately, systems are dumb—not dumb as in stupid, just passive. Inert. They can spit out data until the cows come home, but none of it matters until some people get together to discuss what the data means and what to do about it. Dialogue is what determines whether we execute the right actions at the right time in the right way. Systems are just a support mechanism.

Better Dialogue, Better Operating System

I hope you can now see that every decision your organization makes, every project it launches, and every employee it hires, is only as good as the dialogue that preceded that action. In that way, dialogue really is your company's operating system. It's the network through which all perspectives, information, insights, ideas, and challenges flow.

> Every decision your organization makes, every project it launches, and every employee it hires, is only as good as the dialogue that preceded that action.

By contrast, your business processes (budgeting, recruiting, business reviews, account planning) are like apps. They each require some intelligence, and they can each be good or bad, but they can only ever be as good as the operating system they run on. If your operating system is weak, it's certain to drag down the effectiveness of all your apps.

That's why great dialogue beats great systems every time. If you took over a company with excellent systems but terrible communication, it wouldn't take long for those systems to be spewing red alerts all over the place. On the other hand, if the company had terrible systems (or no systems) but great dialogue, problems would still get solved—including the problem of how to build great systems.

Systems can't fix people, but people can fix systems.

Systems can't fix people, but people can fix systems.

In a Day Zero organization, there are no systems but plenty of great dialogue. As your company grows, you'll build lots of systems, which are necessary for your organization to scale. But as you wrestle with the information they produce, it will be the quality of your dialogue that determines the outcome, much more than the quality of the systems themselves.

The risk is that the quality of your dialogue deteriorates as you scale—due to the exponential growth of complexity in your organization. It's natural for the quality of dialogue to fall off over time . . . unless you're proactively doing something to prevent that, which is precisely what this book is about.

Recap

- Conversations are the foundation of your company, more so than money or ideas. The quality of conversations you have ultimately determines the quality of the products, strategies, and decisions you make.

- Dialogue is not just speaking and listening; it's the act of learning and thinking together, which we can also call collective thinking.

- Collective thinking leads to better ideas, solutions, and decisions. It also leads to a deeper commitment to the decisions that are taken and high levels of engagement and satisfaction.

- Everyone has a different perspective. The right/wrong frame hinders collective thinking and often results in unproductive debates. Reframing with intellectual humility, assuming both parties are partly right, promotes collective thinking.

- The ladder of inference explains how we reach our conclusions. By sharing and comparing our ladders, we can understand different perspectives and find better solutions.

- The Thinking Together Ritual involves deep listening, asking questions, and understanding each other's perspectives. It helps harness collective intelligence and leads to discussions that are both Productive and Positive.

Chapter 4

Training Doesn't Work . . . Rituals Do

▼

This chapter explores what makes real change so hard and why rituals unlock sustainable change in your organization.

CONVERSATIONS ARE TAKING PLACE THROUGHOUT your organization. Colleagues chatting over how to approach a particular problem. Managers delegating new tasks to their people or sharing feedback. Meetings of all kinds, including updates, business reviews, budget sessions, and strategy sessions. Each of those conversations represents an opportunity: a chance for people to generate new ideas and make solid decisions, and to do so in a way that leaves everyone motivated, engaged, and feeling good about their team and the culture of the organization. Or not.

If you could measure all the conversations taking place across the whole of your organization and plot the results on the Productivity and Positivity matrix (page 62), what do you think it would look like? I'm sure you'd find plenty of room for improvement. And for that to happen, your people will need to develop some new skills. The question is how best to accomplish that.

Is the answer . . . training?

Training promises to upgrade your skills in a short amount of time, and who wouldn't want that? The problem is that training doesn't work. We've always known that, and it's even more true in a rapidly scaling business for three reasons:

1. **Training isn't sticky.** While it may have an impact on people's skill levels for a short time, training typically has a decay curve, where people soon forget the tools and techniques they've learned and go back to their previous ways.

2. **Training isn't viral.** If you're a high-growth company, you're hiring new people all the time, opening new offices, and bringing in remote workers. It takes a tremendous amount of money, time, and discipline to sustain the level of training required to keep everyone's skills up to the level you're looking for.

3. **Business is stressful.** Working in a rapidly growing company is even more stressful. While it's relatively easy to have conversations that are both Productive and Positive when the stakes are low—for example, when we're deciding where to hold the company picnic—these aren't the conversations that matter. By definition, the conversations that matter most to your company's performance (Productivity) and to the lived experience of your people (Positivity) are stressful ones. Unfortunately, it's a lot harder to learn to maintain high Productivity and Positivity in these situations, and this is when training falls especially short.

To understand why, consider management theorist Martin Broadwell's four stages of competence.

1. **Unconscious incompetence.** You're doing it poorly but don't realize it.
2. **Conscious incompetence.** You're aware that you're doing it poorly.
3. **Conscious competence.** You can do it well when you focus on it, but it doesn't come naturally.
4. **Unconscious competence.** You do it well without having to think about it.

Training can only ever get you to level three. But in the heat of battle—when things aren't going according to plan or critical decisions need to be made—conscious competence isn't enough.

> **In the heat of battle—when things aren't going according to plan or critical decisions need to be made—conscious competence isn't enough.**

Blame the amygdala. At times like these, it floods your body with stress hormones, which can overwhelm the logical thinking that takes place in your frontal cortex. If the stress levels are low, your logical self might win out, but as they rise, you're unlikely to remember—or use—all those skills you were "trained" in.

That's why military organizations drill basic procedures over and over. They know that when the first bullet flies, a soldier's logical thinking goes out the window. If you're in mortal danger and can't think how to load your weapon, what good was all that training? Knowing how to do it right isn't enough—it has to become almost reflexive, a deeply ingrained habit.

It's the same—although hopefully less life-threatening—in business. Holding conversations that are Productive and Positive in the heat of battle can only happen if the skills and behaviors that produce them have become deeply ingrained habits for your people.

How do we go from conscious competence to habit? Through the repeated practice that comes from rituals.

The Walk and Talk Ritual

When I first entered the offices of PayStep, a Dutch fintech company handling B2B payments, I sensed something unique about its culture. There was an undeniable energy and a style of open communication that started with the receptionist—who knew from the moment I entered who I was, why I was there, and whom I was going to meet—all the way up to Stefan, their founder and CEO.

This was fifteen years ago, long before I'd developed the rituals in this book. At the time, I was just starting to help companies improve team dynamics and break down silos—but PayStep didn't have these problems. Instead, what Stefan and his cofounders, Anneke and Menno, wanted was for me to help them "bottle their magic" so they wouldn't lose it as they grew.

PayStep was still a small Day Zero organization, and the founders hadn't felt the need to formalize anything about their culture. But they knew they were about to go through a major growth spurt, so they asked me to help them distill what was unique about their culture and find a way to embed it in the daily life of their people.

We set off for a weekend at Stefan's parents' house in the forest outside the Hague to work. Fueled by Chinese takeout, we spent the next two days discussing what had made PayStep the way it was and how to keep it going.

The three founders had come from different backgrounds—Stefan had been an investment banker, Anneke was from consulting, and Menno had been in software development. They wanted to take the best from each of their backgrounds and discard the worst.

Anneke went first. She had loved the collegiality of her time in consulting and the focus on joint problem-solving rather than on a hierarchical approach to decision-making. While at her firm, she had also been exposed to the ideas of Chris Argyris, founder of the "learning organization" concept and inventor of the ladder of inference.

This led us to the first core principle: learning. We agreed that when discussions generated new learning for everyone involved, people naturally became more aligned and worked better together.

But we wanted something simple and catchy to embody these lofty ideals, and the question we eventually settled on was "What did we learn?" The idea was this: When people have different perspectives about an issue (which they always do), it's not enough for them to resolve their differences—they should be able to say what they learned from each other through the course of their discussions and how that influenced their thinking. That would help them to become better listeners to really understand the other person's point of view and to argue their own point based on logic and data, not political or hierarchical power.

Stefan's experience in investment banking, as well as his time as an elite rower, had made him extremely performance oriented, so he wanted something to capture that. We settled on the "Will it make the boat go faster?" concept developed by Olympic gold medalist–rower Ben Hunt-Davis. The principle is simple: every decision should be viewed through the lens of whether it would make the boat—in this case, the business—go faster.

The third principle was particularly important to Menno. He had previously worked for a company that employed the polder model, a highly collaborative, consensus-oriented approach to management. The model is named after the Dutch word *polder*, which refers to a piece of land that has been reclaimed from the sea. In a polder, the dikes are maintained collectively by the various farmers who own land within the polder. Menno had seen firsthand the way this kind of a culture led to better collaboration and had brought that to PayStep, and his colleagues all wanted to make sure they didn't lose it as PayStep grew.

This approach made a lot of sense to Stefan as well, since he had rowed in an eight: a boat with eight rowers plus a coxswain. How strong each rower was and how hard he pulled was only a part of the overall success. If all eight weren't pulling in perfect unison, they were bound to lose. The question that emerged to capture this principle was "How can we row better together?"

Having set out these core principles, we then discussed how they could embed them—make them sticky and, ideally, viral. We agreed that an element of training was important but not nearly enough. We were looking for a way to embed these principles so deeply into the culture that people wouldn't have to think about them.

The PayStep team had developed the habit of holding many of their discussions while walking around their office building. Anneke thought that the physical movement and cold air stimulated sharp and creative thinking, and Stefan liked the fact that it kept people from sitting around in meetings longer than they needed to (thanks to the cold and wet weather). We decided to build on that and came up with a ritual we called Walk and Talk.

Here's how it worked. Whenever people were making an important decision, or when a thorny topic, conflict, or disagreement arose, the folks involved would discuss it as they walked around the office complex—up to a maximum of three loops. Each loop took fifteen to twenty minutes.

On the first loop, the focus was on the first principle, learning: What did each person know or understand that the others needed to understand? Who had the most relevant data or analysis, and what did it tell them? Who had the best way of looking at the problem?

The second loop concentrated on the question of what would make the boat go faster. The focus now was to consider what decision or approach would drive the fastest growth of the company.

On the third loop, the focus was on how to row better together. In practice, this meant two things: What should they do to ensure smooth progress going forward—who else needed to buy in, what obstacles might they encounter, what objections might people have, and how could these be addressed? The other aspect was: How could they have worked better together up until this point? If there had been a friction, what could have prevented it?

Finally, if they still couldn't resolve the issue after three loops, they could ask one of the cofounders to join as a coxswain—someone to facilitate the discussion and coach them to an outcome—or when all else failed, to just make the call.

Stefan insisted on tracking the results, and one year later, this is what he found: 30 percent of the Walk and Talk sessions wrapped up successfully in one or two loops. Including the sessions that ran three loops, more than 93 percent of Walk and Talks had led to a successful outcome without the need for a coxswain. The last 7 percent used a coxswain to come to closure.

And that is how my first ritual was born fifteen years ago.

Rituals Are Pathways

The limits of the Walk and Talk ritual are of course obvious—in today's world of remote work and global business, anything that requires us to be in the same place isn't going to work, much less scale. So, it was no surprise when I got a call from Stefan a couple of years later saying they needed to reinvent the approach and asking whether I could help. By then, they had over one hundred employees and were planning on a second office, so it was time to find new ways of embedding their core principles into the company culture.

When I visited, I found that many people were still using the ritual, but others weren't. I interviewed a range of people including both religious users of Walk and Talk and those who had dropped it. When I asked the droppers about their experience, they told me that they had tried to stick to it, but when it became impractical and they stopped using it, they'd noticed that they just didn't need it any longer. They felt that the conversations they held in the office were just as good as those held in the cold rain. Working based on the core principles had become a habit.

At that moment, the penny dropped. By this time, I'd been teaching leadership, management, and collaboration skills for a number of years. I was confident I'd had an impact on my clients, but I still had my lingering concerns: Would these skills stick as the company grew? Could they go viral and spread to people who had never been trained? And would people use them even when the *stakes were high* and they were super stressed?

My experience with PayStep showed me that the answer

to these questions came down to a single word: *habits*. If you want to make a real impact on your organization's effectiveness, teaching your people key skills isn't enough. You need to find a way to translate these skills into habits—and that's where rituals come in. If you practice a ritual for a while, sooner or later you'll find that the skills embedded in it are there for you to draw on without having to think about them.

Rituals are the pathway that leads from skills to habits.

Recap

- Traditional approaches to training don't embed skills deeply enough to really make a difference.

- We can all be at our best in low-stress situations. But it's how we handle conflict, sensitive issues, and high-stakes situations (when we and others may be stressed) that matters the most.

- For us to be at our best in these situations, we need to turn our communication skills into deeply ingrained habits.

- The way to do this—and to generate long-term improvement in your organization's effectiveness—is by practicing rituals, which act as pathways from skills to habits.

- PayStep's Walk and Talk ritual demonstrates how even one simple ritual can transform an organization.

Chapter 5

Getting Started

▼

This chapter shares nine tips on how to get started using this program.

IN THE FOLLOWING CHAPTERS, I will share nineteen additional friction-busting and culture-building rituals in addition to the one I've already shared. These are designed to be easy to learn, share, and incorporate into the daily flow of your organization's work. As a leader, your first role is to master them, and then to teach by example. Your next goal is to become their champion and spread them across your company.

By practicing these rituals, your people will develop the habit of engaging in high Productivity and Positivity dialogue in everything they do. This will help them prevent frictions from building up and resolve them quickly when they do crop up. By spreading these across your organization, you'll be able to maintain high-performance as you scale. But before we dive in, let me offer a few tips.

Tip 1: Start at the Top—with Yourself

As senior leaders, we often treat development as something that our junior and midlevel people need—but surely not us! Because we've been successful, we are at risk of assuming that we have all the skills we need. Or we might feel that our time is just too valuable to take our focus away from the day-to-day . . . but this is shortsighted.

As we know, even the star athletes on the top sports teams hit the gym. They still do their squats and lunges. It's how they maintain their fitness and boost their ability to perform under even the toughest conditions. The same goes for you and your senior leaders. You may think your leadership skills are already there, and they may well be. But we can all learn.

But there's one more reason to start with yourself. You're probably familiar with the idea that you haven't fully mastered a topic until you can teach it to someone else. I believe this applies to leadership as well. I have worked with many executives who had terrific natural leadership skills—but they weren't able to articulate why they did the things they did or what the underlying principles were. That made them excellent leaders but not very good teachers. By learning the frameworks and approaches that underpinned their natural skills—that is, by turning implicit knowledge into explicit knowledge—these executives became much more effective at teaching and transferring their skills to others.

Tip 2: Start Now

As your grandmother may have said, an ounce of prevention is worth a pound of cure. The point of these rituals is to prevent frictions, not just to fix them. You may not think your organization has many problems, which makes it easy to postpone this program so that you can focus on more "urgent" issues. But even if you do have a healthy organization, now is the perfect time to start practicing these skills—before problems have taken hold. And, as we saw, if you're scaling, the problems will come.

If you think about the rituals as the basis for maintaining your organization's fitness—the squats and lunges that will keep it performing at its best—starting now makes sense. If you think about them as a way to create the habits you'll need to scale successfully, starting now becomes imperative.

Tip 3: Start with One or Two Rituals—but Really Master Them

Time is short for all of us, and I recognize that mastering anything new takes a lot of time and energy. I suggest you start by focusing a few of the core rituals, including Thinking Together (page 55) and the rituals in chapter 6. Practice these to the point that they become unconscious habits, at which point they no longer take up your time and energy and you can move on to some other rituals.

Tip 4: Check Your Organizational Health

I recommend that you run my organizational health survey, which you can find by using the following QR code. It can be used either at a departmental- or company-wide level. The results will give you a clear sense of where to start, and you'll also have a baseline against which you can measure ongoing improvement.

Scan this QR code to get my detailed guide to measuring your organization's health.

Tip 5: Emphasize Quality of Practice

The speed at which you and your colleagues make progress is as much a function of the quality of your practice as the repetition. It's a good idea to take a half day or day offsite with your team to kick-start the work so that you can all be 100 percent focused.

Tip 6: Leverage Social Learning

It's always a good idea to teach these skills to intact teams wherever possible. That way everyone can encourage and remind each other to use them, as well as serve as role models for each other.

Tip 7: Scale the Change

Just as it takes thought and effort to scale your business, it's going to take some focused effort to scale the introduction of these rituals beyond you and your immediate team so that they reach the whole of your organization. You'll want to appoint an internal champion who has a passion for this work, and you may also want to enlist the help of a coach.

Tip 8: Make Them Your Own

You'll be relieved to know that none of the rituals involve long walks outside in the cold rain. The magic is not so much in the precise design of any one ritual as it is in conscious practice. Just as you need to know the rules before you can break them, I suggest you master these rituals as they are set out in this book. Once you have done so, I encourage you to adapt them and make them your own.

Tip 9: Keep the Faith

Eventually, these rituals will become so integrated into your culture that new employees will pick them up naturally, without training, just by watching and copying the behavior of others around them. If you've ever worked for a company with a superstrong culture, you'll know that this can happen. Keep the faith in the early days, and you'll reap the benefits for many years to come.

Recap

- Most rituals can be incorporated into your daily flow of work.

- As a leader, your role is to role-model use of the rituals and to encourage others to use them.

- Practicing the rituals will enable you to generate consistently Productive and Positive interactions.

- Once you've mastered the art of that, you'll no longer need to remember the rituals themselves; they will come naturally.

Chapter 6

Trust
Building Rituals

▼

In this chapter, we'll learn why a certain type of trust underpins all healthy organizations and how your people can proactively develop this trust in all their relationships.

M OST PEOPLE INTUITIVELY GET that trust is the foundation of all great working relationships. The problem is that we don't always know what kind of trust we'll need, how much, or when we'll need it. And we can't just switch trust on when we need it. It's a process that takes time to develop.

Most people are okay with allowing the trust with their coworkers to evolve slowly and organically. I believe we should be taking a different approach: actively cultivating trust from the very start and carefully tending to it when it is in danger of being damaged. This chapter is all about why trust is central to building a high-performance organization and how you can do so.

What Is Trust?

First, let's define what we mean by trust. I'm not talking about transactional trust, which is the feeling that someone is reliable, and that you can count on them to do what they say they will do. Transactional trust is important, but it's not nearly enough. I'm talking about relational (or interpersonal) trust: the feeling that you have an emotional connection with someone. That you can open up and be vulnerable with them. That they will support you and have your back in a difficult situation. That they have good intentions and will act with integrity. And, importantly, that you can share difficult truths with them and have that be okay.

Transactional trust is important, but it's not nearly enough.

When two colleagues work closely together—as in a Day Zero organization—they don't think about the need to consciously build relational trust. That's because it tends to grow naturally, largely as a result of the many informal chats they'll have, perhaps over coffee or lunch. These chats typically stray well beyond work topics into areas such as kids, family, outings, holidays, sports, and more. These allow people to get to know each other at a more personal level—they're the easiest and most elemental "us" conversations.

This laissez-faire approach works up to a point, but it doesn't always generate the depth of trust we need to navigate challenging situations—which we'll talk more about later. But nothing has done more to highlight the need for us to stop relying on this organic approach than the recent explosion in remote work. Even brand-new start-ups—companies that should be reaping all the benefits of a Day Zero organization—are finding that most of these advantages have been lost as a result of operating partly or fully remote. Why? Because they're no longer having those lunch or coffee chats. Their opportunities to build relational trust through "us" conversations have been dramatically curtailed.

What We Talk About—and What We Don't

If you look around your organization, you'll find that everyone is busy happily discussing thousands of "it" issues: budgets, projects, milestones, work plans, products, sales figures. But you will also see everyone trying as hard as possible to avoid discussing all manner of "us" issues: uncomfortable team dynamics, toxic behavior, the manager who "shits down but kisses up," and even the regular day-to-day feedback that people need and deserve.

All these "us" topics are pointing at *interpersonal* tensions that have cropped up in your organization. Whether at work or at home, it's inevitable that tensions will crop up in any relationship, even our best ones. Tensions aren't inherently good or bad; they're just a part of life. But whether you address them—and how well that goes—determines whether your relational trust spikes upward or falls off a cliff. And when tensions go unresolved, they eat away at trust and lead to silos, lack of collaboration, petty politics, and other behaviors that slow your organization down.

Tensions and Niggles

A *tension* is any issue important enough that you would really like to resolve it through having a constructive conversation with the other person. It's different from a niggle. A *niggle* is something that bothers you for a little while but that soon fades away. A tension is something that is likely to continue to bother you, at least for some time. Let's say your colleague interrupted you a couple of times in a meeting—that's probably a niggle, not a big enough deal that you'd feel the need to discuss it. But if they also dismissed your ideas in a way that you found disrespectful, it might bother you a lot more. Left undiscussed, it's likely to change the way you feel toward them—and to interfere with future collaboration.

Assuming you value your relationship with this person—which you should if you may need to work with them in the future—you'd ideally want to have a conversation to put the tension to bed so that your relationship isn't negatively affected. This is an "us" conversation of a wholly different type than the easy "get to know each other" coffee chats. This requires a much deeper level of trust to even get started.

The first question is, will you have that conversation?

The only way to resolve these tensions and get your organization running smoothly and friction-free is to have a (successful) "us" conversation. That's completely possible—in fact, my main message to you is that you should assume that it's far easier than you imagine. But there are some barriers, so it's important that we understand what those barriers are and how we can remove them.

The AI Program That Makes "Us" Conversations So Hard

Getting to know someone over lunch—asking about their kids or hobbies or discussing mutual interests—is about as easy as a conversation gets. These types of "us" conversations build interpersonal trust but at a very gentle pace.

Other types of "us" conversations are different. Calling out someone's unhelpful behavior or surfacing uncomfortable team dynamics, for example, are both much more challenging topics to discuss—but important ones to address if you're going to have a healthy organization. Even the simple task of giving someone feedback—for example, letting them know how something they did or said made you feel—can be hard. Why is this?

Because we all have a little AI program in our heads that filters what comes out of our mouths. Its job is to make sure we don't say anything that would offend, embarrass, or upset others, or to expose ourselves to embarrassment or criticism. In other words, this AI program is there to keep things safe and comfortable—to prevent us from taking interpersonal risk—so that our relationships won't be damaged. This program runs constantly, in the background, so we don't generally notice what it has chosen to filter out.

We also don't have a clear view of how it's calibrated. When we trust someone deeply, we're much more comfortable raising potentially awkward issues. But when trust is low or neutral, we filter more—a *lot* more.

If you look around your organization, you'll see that it has three buckets of topics. Bucket 1 holds the topics people happily discuss openly with their colleagues—99 percent of these are "it" topics.

Bucket 2 holds the topics that some people discuss—but only with their trusted friends, and often only at the bar. This bucket is full of "us" topics. This is where we talk about the tensions we're experiencing and desperately want to resolve but don't know how. As a result, this is where gossip lives and frustrations fester. In short, bucket 2 is full of important topics, but these topics rarely get addressed and resolved in an effective way. If you think about your own buckets, you'll find there's probably plenty in bucket 2!

And then there's bucket 3, which contains topics so sensitive that we don't talk about them at all, not even with friends—these are the classic elephants too big to mention, the emperors with no clothes. Most healthy organizations have very small bucket 3s, but even the healthiest have huge bucket 2s.

Buckets 2 and 3 are a huge problem for a simple but profound reason: *we can't solve a problem if we can't talk about it.* As we saw, "us" conversations typically refer to a tension in the organization. So, if we can't talk about the tension, then we can't resolve it—and if we can't resolve it, then tensions proliferate. Frictions grow. Motivation drops. Performance deteriorates. And your organization slows down.

We can't solve a problem if we can't talk about it.

Buckets 2 and 3 are where Productivity and Positivity go to die.

The Trap We're In

Perhaps you've already spotted the trap we find ourselves in. We can't solve our tension if we can't talk about it. But if we don't talk about it, trust between us will go down—so we're caught in a vicious cycle.

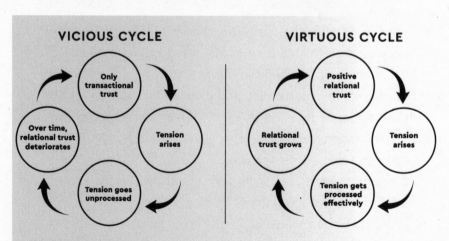

Figure 6.1. The vicious and virtuous cycles.

If, on the other hand, we can talk about it and resolve it in a constructive way, then trust shoots up—now we're in a virtuous circle.

But how do we get out of the vicious cycle?

The key is to recognize that trust is conditional—specifically, it's a function of how much risk we've navigated and how that process has gone. Imagine that I'm an active mountain climber and you're someone who wants to get into the sport. We can start by going for some local hikes nearby. But if I then mention that I'm planning to climb Everest and ask if you'd like to come along, are you going to? If the hardest thing we've done together is take a walk in the local foothills, you definitely won't feel safe. It's not that you don't trust me, but you don't trust me enough *for that level of risk*—so you'd almost certainly skip the trip. If, on the other hand, we've had a chance to work our way up to climbing bigger and more challenging mountains over the past few years, and you've had a chance to see what a calm and experienced mountain guide I am, then you'll be a lot more willing to follow me up Everest.

In work, as in mountain climbing, the depth of trust we have with someone is proportional to the *degree of risk* we have navigated with them—as well as how that navigation process has gone.

Trust is what enables us to start up these mountains called interpersonal frictions. Skill is what enables us to navigate them successfully. And the rest of this chapter is devoted to equipping you with the skills you need.

From Tensions to Trust

Here's the trap, one more time, in visual form. This will help you understand more deeply how to avoid the vicious cycle and get into a virtuous circle.

Case 1: We became coworkers recently. We've hung out a little, and a bit of interpersonal trust has grown organically. But it's below the "Everest threshold" where I'm willing to have a difficult conversation with you. So, when a tension arises, I don't raise the topic, and we don't resolve the tension. I still like you, and we work well enough together, but when another small tension arises that I also don't address, these slowly chip away at our working relationship. You'll never be my favorite colleague.

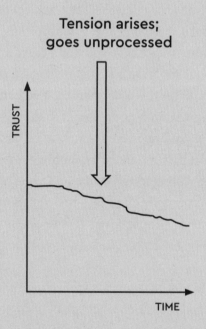

Figure 6.2. What happens when a tension arises and goes unprocessed.

Case 2: We've worked together for a while but only remotely. We've had no chance to build any meaningful interpersonal trust, and I haven't seen any reason to do so. You've been fine on the transactional trust side, and that's all I care about. But then you did something that really pissed me off. Unlike some people in this company, I believe in facing things head-on. So, I called you and really let you have it. I made it very clear that I won't tolerate this kind of behavior. Unfortunately, I hadn't taken the time to understand the situation you were in or the reasons you had for what you did. So, you became angry and told me I don't know what I'm talking about. In short, the conversation went extremely poorly. Now, our trust has fallen off a cliff. We're unlikely to ever talk about anything risky again, certainly not in an open and constructive way. Our relationship has become a point of friction that the rest of the organization will just need to work around.

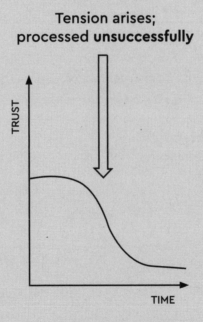

Figure 6.3. What happens when a tension arises and is processed unsuccessfully.

To break out of this vicious cycle, we need to build our trust by having deeper "us" conversations (not just about our kids)—*before* any tensions have cropped up. As we'll see, our second ritual—Share Your Personal User Guide (PUG)—is an *easy, zero-risk* way of kick-starting relational trust. Once you've run through this, it will be much easier for you to process tensions or hold any other "us" conversations you need to have down the road. In fact, I've seen this simple ritual dramatically transform the trust among colleagues and across teams.

Case 3: Now we start with neutral trust—but thanks to sharing our PUG, our trust level is above the threshold. So, when a tension came up, I felt comfortable raising it. Using the Turning Tensions into Trust Ritual (page 101), our conversation went well—and we acknowledged that, while it wasn't entirely easy or comfortable, we're much better off having had that conversation, and we recognize the impact on our trust that it has had. Now we're becoming besties. And we're confident we can tackle any future tensions without a hitch.

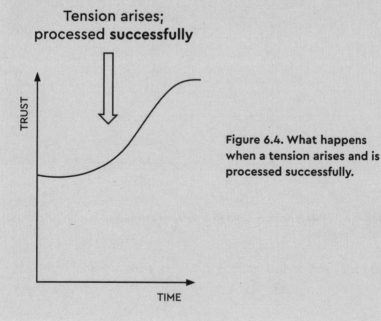

**Tension arises;
processed successfully**

Figure 6.4. What happens when a tension arises and is processed successfully.

Your Role as a Leader

Leaders have a responsibility for keeping the number of issues in bucket 2 down to a minimum. You can never get rid of them completely, as new tensions are always arising, but if you don't pay attention to this, then the tensions slopping around in buckets 2 and 3 will grow into frictions that will eventually slow you down.

One way to think about your role in this is as a trust coach. If you ask anyone in your organization to plot their key working relationships on a trust spectrum ranging from mistrust (or low), through neutral, up to high, you're probably going to see a classic bell curve—perhaps one that is skewed a bit to the right, as it is in figure 6.5.

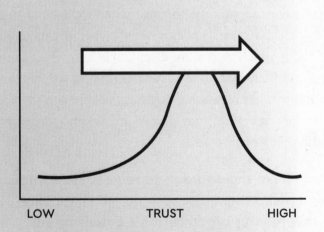

LOW   TRUST   HIGH

Figure 6.5. Our working relationships range from low to high trust. Wouldn't it be great if we could systematically move them all to the right?

Whether your people are sitting around a kitchen table or working from all around the world, your job is to help them get out of the laissez-faire approach to building trust and into a more intentional and proactive mindset. Creating a culture in which people are encouraged to shift their bell curves systematically to the right, through the use of PUGs, is a great first step.

But there's more that you can do. Because not all tensions are interpersonal in nature—some run throughout the entire organization. These are the proverbial elephants in the room that no one wants to talk about. They can take many forms but might include aspects of your company's financial performance or stability, the lack of success you're having with a particular product or customer, the high turnover in a particular department, or the lack of diversity in your management team. These are all classic bucket 2 and bucket 3 topics, and it's natural that people are reluctant to raise them. But as a leader, you can make a huge difference here.

If you have the courage to raise these topics and make them discussable, you'll quickly rewire your organization's beliefs about which topics are discussable and which aren't. You might initially be scared to raise them yourself, but don't forget that you're not sharing anything people don't already know. In fact, many of your people *are already talking about these topics—at the bar!*

If you have the courage to raise these topics and make them discussable, you'll quickly rewire your organization's beliefs about which topics are discussable and which aren't.

The moment you name one of these, you might briefly feel the tension rise in the room—"Did he just set off a bomb?" Yet just a second later, you'll feel the tension ease. No bombs went off. No dead babies fell from the sky. Everyone already knew about the issue—there's no new news here—but now you're in a position to talk about it openly to clarify misconceptions, share important information, give relevant context, and demonstrate that management is not clueless or putting its head in the sand, but rather recognizes the issue and is doing its best to address it.

Now a constructive dialogue can begin. In my many years of coaching teams, I can't remember any situations in which leaders surfacing bucket 2 topics didn't lead to a good outcome, as long as the leader managed the conversation skillfully.

Over time, your people will internalize that these conversations aren't nearly as scary as they had imagined, and soon they'll also be surfacing bucket 2 topics. Now you've created a culture in which we *can name the problem* so we can solve it. And now you're on the way to building a healthy, scalable, and friction-free organization.

Ritual 2:
Share Your Personal User Guide (PUG)

In this ritual, you create and share a narrative about who you are as a colleague and how others can work most effectively with you, get the best out of you, and avoid the worst. I call this your personal user guide (PUG), and it's proved hugely helpful for many of my clients.

Step 1: Determine your working style. There are many frameworks that can help you understand your working style, including famous ones such as the Myers-Briggs Type Indicator (MBTI), DISC assessments, and CliftonStrengths. Feel free to use whichever framework you prefer. Personally, I find the PSIU framework developed by Lex Sisney, an expert in organizational design, extremely simple yet insightful. The PSIU uses four working styles: Producer, Stabilizer, Unifier, and Innovator. Everyone has all four styles to some degree, but typically one will dominate.

- **Producers (P)** have a high drive to achieve results, move at a fast pace, and tend to take a short-term view. They are focused on *what they can accomplish now*; they want to get started straight away and work hard to accomplish goals quickly.

- **Stabilizers (S)** are process oriented and prefer to follow a structured approach. They are focused on *how to do things "right"* or reliably. Stabilizers like to plan carefully before making decisions. They are generally highly organized and pay close attention to detail.

- **Innovators (I)** move at a fast pace and are results oriented like Producers but operate in a more creative and less structured way. They are focused on finding *new and better ways of doing things*. Innovators are creative, big-picture people who have lots of new ideas and are excited by the latest one.

- **Unifiers (U)** are focused on *who should be involved and how to bring them together*. They think deeply about team building and encouraging strong, healthy relationships.

While anyone can work outside their natural style, it comes less naturally. For example, imagine asking one of your most innovative people to look after the bookkeeping for a few days. They may be able and willing to do it, but they're likely to be bored and restless. But if you asked them to find a faster and simpler way for the company to keep the books, it would unleash their creativity and possibly result in a dramatically better outcome.

Lex Sisney uses the following story to help people find their most natural style: Imagine that you gather sixteen people together, four of each working style, and divide them into their respective groups. Each team is given the challenge of rowing across a lake in the shortest amount of time.

As soon as you say "Start," the **Producers** will jump in their boat and start rowing, hard and fast. They won't ask questions or focus on the process. The **Stabilizers** will start by planning: How far is it to cross the lake? How long is it likely to take? How many breaks should we take, and when? What is the best route? How will the winds and currents affect us? Only after everything has been planned will they start to row. When the **Innovators** get together, they'll start to come up with new ideas: Why don't we put a sail on this baby? How about a better rowing mechanism? Come to think of it, a 150-HP motor would do the trick; I bet we can find one at the marina. The **Unifiers** will start with a team bonding session. They'll develop a team cheer and agree about how they will help each other if anyone gets overly tired. Then they'll head off. Most people look at these four working styles and immediately identify most strongly with one of them.

Step 2: Draft your personal user guide (PUG). Write your answers to the following questions and give examples wherever possible. This list isn't necessarily exhaustive, so feel free to add any information that might help others work well with you.

- What are your working-style preferences based on the PSIU framework? How do these show up?
- What are the implications of your style preference for how you work best with others?
- What are your greatest strengths, and how can people best take advantage of them?

- Which of your strengths do you tend to overuse? How does this show up? What is the potential impact of this on others?

- What do people often misunderstand about you? How would you want them to think about this aspect of you?

- What else have people told you is difficult about working with you?

- What are one or two things that trigger you (cause you to become upset or defensive)?

- What else should people know about you to work well with you?

- Based on your answers to the questions above, what are you committed to improving or changing?

- How can others help you with this? What would you particularly welcome feedback on?

Step 3: Refine your PUG. Share your PUG with a couple of colleagues who know you well and ask them what might be inaccurate or missing. Incorporate their feedback before sharing it more broadly.

Step 4: Share your PUG with a colleague. Get together with any colleague you want to build Relational trust with. Allow about an hour for this exercise. Decide who will go first to share their PUG. Then have that person ask the following questions:

- Is there anything in my PUG that doesn't ring true? What aspects do you see differently?

- What is missing?

- Do you have any thoughts about how I can improve in the area I just mentioned?

Step 5: Reverse roles. Now, reverse roles and repeat the questions above. Finally, discuss this final question: Based on what we now know, what should we do to work more effectively together in the future?

I strongly recommend that you use the PUG Ritual when onboarding new employees, forming or changing teams, or kick-starting any cross-functional collaborations between people who haven't previously worked together. It's an excellent way to jump-start the trust building process. It's also a signal to everyone that "us" conversations are a normal, essential, and not-so-scary part of doing business.

You only need to prepare your PUG once, but each time you share it, you should learn a little more about yourself, allowing you to fine-tune it over time. By the time you've shared it five or ten times, your PUG is such an accurate and nuanced reflection of who you are and what it's like to work with you that the people you share it with will immediately get you—and also see you as a highly self-aware person.

Ritual 3:
Turning Tensions into Trust

Hopefully sharing your PUG has helped you get off to a good start in building high-trust relationships with your colleagues. But even in the best of relationships, tensions crop up. They're an inevitable part of life. Any tension that might interfere with your ability to collaborate perfectly together in the future is worth addressing. This ritual helps you to do that in a safe and comfortable way.

Step 1: Set up a conversation. When there is a tension to resolve, find a suitable time to talk about it: "I'd like to talk about something that happened in yesterday's meeting. I'm hoping we can have an open and constructive conversation—is now a good time?"

Step 2: Name the source of the tension—say what you saw—and how it made you feel. Make sure you stick to completely observable behaviors that could have been captured by a video. What did the person do or say that's bothering you? If you aren't exactly sure what they did (for example, you heard about it through a third party), share what you heard and ask them to clarify what actually took place.

Be careful to avoid saying anything that attributes blame. And don't speculate about their motives for doing what they did. Just say what happened and how it made you feel: "Several times in the past few team meetings, you've interrupted me while I was talking about my project. When that happens, I get flustered, and I also feel undermined."

Step 3: Acknowledge your possible contribution. The great risk is that the conversation becomes a blame-fest—which is exactly what you don't want to happen. The surest way to avoid that is by starting with anything at all that you did (or failed to do) that might have helped create the tension—*even if you feel that your contribution was by far the smaller part*. That keeps the other person from jumping into defense mode and shows them that you've entered the conversation in good faith. You're there to make things right, not to cast blame. Try: "I know that I sometimes go on too long about my project. Do you have any suggestions for how I could tighten up my reports? Is there anything else I could do to be more effective at these meetings?" Ask them for their thoughts about that and whether they see anything else you could do differently.

Step 4: Find out how they see it. Restate your concern and find out how they see what happened. What were they trying to achieve at that time? Ask those questions and listen closely to the answers. Don't interrupt! You might hear something you didn't expect. Try: "I want to come back to the interruptions. Were you aware that you were doing this? How did you experience this meeting?"

Now use the skills you learned in the Thinking Together Ritual (page 55): stay quiet, grow curious, and listen attentively to whatever they say. Under no circumstance should you interrupt—even if you don't agree with their perspective.

Step 5: Acknowledge their point of view and make a request. What makes sense to you about what they said or how they see the situation? What is still uncomfortable or unresolved for you? What can you do to make it better, and what is something practical you'd like them to do? Try: "I hear you. We had a lot on the agenda and time was short. I agree that in the future I should leave most of the details out of my project update. About the interrupting, I know you had no bad intention, but I wouldn't want it to happen again. I'll do my best to keep my reports concise, but if you think I'm still going on too long, please just let me know afterward rather than cutting me off, okay?"

Step 6: Recognize their goodwill and skill. Thank them for helping to clear the air and for handling the situation well: "I'm really glad we had this conversation, and thanks for making it comfortable and constructive."

Few leaders of high-growth companies spend much time thinking about whether their people are holding invaluable "us" conversations. The assumption is that "it" conversations are the ones that drive results—and that "us" conversations are at best a feel-good factor and at worst a risky and uncomfortable endeavor to be avoided at all costs.

That assumption is wrong. Really wrong. Avoiding "us" conversations means allowing tensions to fester into frictions that slow your company down. A culture in which people regularly surface and resolve bucket 2 issues is a keystone of a high-performance, frictionless organization.

Imagine a world in which, whenever a new employee joins your organization or someone changes teams, no one leaves their full integration to chance. Instead, their onboarding includes sharing PUGs with their closest colleagues. The signal is clear: we value you; and we value open, high-trust relationships. And imagine a world in which tensions that crop up are never left to fester. Everyone knows how to resolve them, not with accusations or blaming but with curiosity, humility, and goodwill. People have learned to work out their issues in a way that builds trust, so relationships are continually deepening. And leaders have no fear of surfacing elephants, trusting that their organizations have developed the maturity to deal with these issues constructively.

Productivity and Positivity are on an unstoppable rise.

Recap

- Trust is essential for building strong working relationships, but it takes time to develop—you can't just switch it on when you need it.

- Transactional trust—trusting that someone can will do what they said they would—is, of course, essential in a high-performance organization.

- But relational trust is even more important. Without it, we can never have the all-important "us" conversations that allow us to resolve tensions and address issues of how we are working together.

- Everyone in your organization should commit to moving all their key working relationships toward increasing levels of interpersonal trust.

- The easiest time to start building relational trust is before any tension has cropped up. The Share Your Personal User Guide Ritual (page 97) gets you started.

- Once a tension has arisen, don't leave it to fester, as that will eventually erode the trust in that relationship. Instead, use the Turning Tensions into Trust Ritual (page 101) to process it. Nothing increases relational trust more than successfully navigating a tension together.

- When your organization systematically avoids "us" conversations, as many do, it leads to a buildup of tensions that ultimately result in silos, factions, broken teams, and other dysfunctions that slow your company down.

- Leaders should have the courage to address elephants in the room and make difficult topics discussable, fostering open dialogue and problem-solving.

Chapter 7

Talent
Building Rituals

▼

*In this chapter, you'll discover why it's so important to develop
great line managers early on and how that can help you successfully scale.*

VIRTUALLY EVERYONE IN YOUR ORGANIZATION has
a manager—and the interactions between people and
their managers have a bigger impact than any other. In fact,
managers are the single biggest shapers of the Productivity,
Positivity, and scalability of your organization.

In a small, stable organization, you can get away with
having a few not-so-good managers. If they're not managing
their people well, you'll hear about it soon enough, and you
can do something about it. And with just a few bad apples,
you won't be setting any cultural norms or precedents that
you can't address later.

But in a scaling organization, it's far more important that
you have consistently high-quality managers. If you have

poor managers, you probably won't know about it for much longer—by which time you may have lost (or switched off) some folks you didn't want to lose. But the bigger problem is the signal you send when you tolerate poor managers and the impact this has on your culture. As your organization grows, people's exposure to the founding or core culture naturally grows weaker. Instead, the lessons they internalize about the behaviors that are tolerated and rewarded increasingly come from the people immediately around them—in particular, their boss.

Managers Drive Positivity

We can't all get what we want all the time. We may not get the raise we hoped for or the desk with a nice view. We may hit the morning traffic jam on the way to work or miss the buzz of the office when we work from home. We may face deadlines that require us to work long, exhausting hours.

All these things can make work life a challenging experience and can undermine our sense of Positivity. But these are facts of life, and it's impossible for employers to solve all these problems.

But there is one thing that every employer should do, and it makes a world of difference: make their people feel validated. And that is largely in the hands of your managers.

During Oprah's last episode, she reflected on what had made her show so successful. Here's what she said:

> I've talked to nearly 30,000 people on this show, and all 30,000 had one thing in common. They all wanted validation ... Every single person you ever will meet shares that common desire: They want to know, do you see me? Do you hear me? Does what I say mean anything to you? Understanding that one principle—that everybody wants to be heard ... has worked for this

platform, and I guarantee you, it will work for yours. Try it with your children, with your husband, your wife, your boss, your friends: Validate them. I see you. I hear you. And what you say matters to me.

"Do you hear me?" and "Does what I say matter to you?" are clear enough. The sad truth is that we all find ourselves in situations—with a customer, a landlord, or a bossy colleague—where we don't feel heard at all. While that's not great behavior on their part, it's not their job to make us feel like our words matter. But it is our manager's job. We all need to feel that we can have some influence. After all, what is the point of my bringing forward my expertise and experience, my hard work and insights, if I know I won't be able to influence anyone? This is a hugely disheartening experience and soon leads to people quietly quitting—showing up but making little effort to contribute.

"Do you see me?" requires a bit more interpretation. I believe what Oprah meant is this: Do you see me as a well-intentioned person? As someone who is doing what they think is best for the company? Or do you see me as a self-serving actor, out to build my empire, cover my ass, look good in front of the boss and throw others under the bus when things go wrong? Sadly, as we will see in more detail in chapter 10, it's part of human nature to make negative assumptions about other people's motives when they do or say things we don't understand. We've all done it about others, and they've done it about us. But if we can establish a high-trust relationship with our manager—one in which they can look past our mistakes and shortcomings and see us as the well-intentioned beings that we all believe we are—then that is a powerful driver of Positivity.

Managers Drive Productivity

Managers determine to a large extent the precise work that gets done, when, by whom, and with what level of oversight. Getting these decisions right can lead to great execution. Get them wrong and Productivity suffers.

One of the toughest challenges managers face in making these calls is determining how much autonomy to give their people. Too much and your people may flail or fail, producing work that isn't what was needed. Too little and they may fail to do their best, take initiative, contribute their best ideas— all signs of demotivation. Either way, the impact on Productivity can be profound.

Effective delegation is the primary tool that managers have for managing autonomy. Delegation sounds simple, but I'm constantly surprised by how poorly understood it is. As a result, it's often a major stumbling point and a source of lost Productivity, especially for inexperienced managers.

The Delegation Dilemma

The first challenge is managers who simply don't delegate when they should. This was the case with François, the COO at a global fintech. François is super smart and always two steps ahead of everyone else. In the short term, he finds it quicker to do things himself than to delegate them to others— and his capacity for work is truly impressive. But, of course, this approach isn't infinitely scalable. As his company grew, tasks and decisions piled up, and he eventually became a bottleneck to progress instead of its primary driver.

The quality of his decisions also suffered, as he had more and more information to process and less and less time in which to do it. When he was operating at 100 percent, they were happy to let him take the lead. Now that he was slowing them down, they just felt disempowered, undervalued, and frustrated. Eventually the company was forced to take some of his responsibilities away—even though he had been their star performer.

The tendency not to delegate what should be delegated is much more common than you'd think. It's not that these managers don't intellectually understand the value of delegation. Rather, their reasons are more subtle. From having surveyed more than two hundred managers who said they had this tendency, it became clear that this mindset was the real barrier. These are among the most frequent reasons they shared with me:

- My people can't do the job as well as I can.
- It's faster for me to do this myself than to explain what I need.
- It takes too much time to train them to bring them up to speed.
- I don't trust them to do it right.
- I like doing it.

These thoughts are largely subconscious. Ask yourself if you ever have thoughts along these lines. If so, you're probably also guilty of not delegating something that you should. A little bit of this is fine—a lot of it and you may end up like François.

Another common mistake managers make when delegating is what I call pulling a Nike—in other words, telling someone to "just do it." By this I mean that they are not giving their people nearly enough context to be successful. The more context you share about why they're being asked to take on a project or task, who else needs to be involved, how this work fits into the bigger picture, what dependencies exist, what has been tried before, and so on, the more likely they are to be both motivated and effective. The Effective Delegation and Aligning on Autonomy Ritual at the end of this chapter will help.

Getting the Right Stage of Autonomy Isn't Easy

Another common mistake managers make is delegating but then micromanaging. This can also have a striking impact on the overall Productivity of your organization; it takes up too much of the manager's time *and* saps the morale of those being managed. Micromanagement can be a real barrier to scaling because managers get bogged down in overseeing today's work when they should be creating tomorrow's.

In recent years, there have been a lot of voices encouraging managers to be more empowering. In fact, the empowerment mantra has taken hold to such an extent that I increasingly find that the biggest factor dragging down Productivity is not micromanagement but its opposite. When managers give too much rope to someone who's not ready for it, it leads to the flail-or-fail syndrome, and this can be a disaster. Let's see why.

Johnson is the CMO of one of Southeast Asia's most successful e-commerce companies. Over the past few years, he built up a team of capable managers who run the various departments within the marketing function: digital, brand, partnerships, comms, PR.

He's a big believer in the idea that by hiring the best people and giving them autonomy, they'll be motivated and produce their best work. But his direction to his people was often so high level that they just weren't clear what he was looking for. As a result, they often floundered. The problem was compounded by the fact that Johnson is a strong introvert, and everyone was working from home during this COVID period, so they had fewer opportunities for informal catchups.

When they eventually presented the work they had done, he was dismissive, saying it had missed the point or that they clearly hadn't understood the strategy or the brief. Weeks of work would get tossed. This pattern continued for some time and eventually became so frustrating that several managers left the company.

When I interviewed Johnson—and many other managers who share the tendency to give too much autonomy—I again heard a subconscious mindset at play. They said things like:

- Deep down, I want my people to like me and say nice things about me, so I don't want to come across as a hard-ass or a micromanager.

- My boss always micromanaged me, and I hated it. I don't want to be like that.

- The best people will figure it out. I know I could.

- In order to attract these very talented people to join, I had to promise them a lot of autonomy—so now I have to live up to my promise.

In summary, there are several subconscious psychological factors acting on managers that make it hard for them to consistently hit the Goldilocks spot where both they and their direct reports feel that the level of delegation, direction, and oversight are "just right." This is in large part because managers have lacked an *explicit framework* for thinking about the different levels of autonomy.

Autonomy Is a Journey

Clearly, the right stage of autonomy for an employee to maximize both their own and their manager's Productivity is not a one-size-fits-all affair. Instead, it's context dependent. An experienced employee doing a routine task in an organization they know well calls for a different approach to delegation and management than a new employee working in a new area on a mission-critical project.

Specifically, the right stage of autonomy depends on the person's *task-relevant experience.* Here are some simple questions that will help you assess what stage of autonomy is appropriate for someone at the time that you're asking them to do something new (i.e., *delegating*):

- How much experience do they have performing this task or something similar?
- Was that experience in this company or a different one?
- Was it while working for you or for someone else?
- Was the context similar or very different?
- Did they generate a high-quality result?

These questions have in them a clue to the critical insight you and your reports need to keep in mind as you work through this process: the right stage of autonomy is constantly evolving.

If you're asking someone to do something they've never done before, or have only done in a very different context, then no matter how much you respect them or how senior they are, *it's perfectly reasonable for you to want to micromanage them—at least to start.* In fact, I would like you to stop thinking of micromanagement as a negative term. It's only negative when it's misapplied. If you're at a new company and you've been given an important job that you're doing for the first time, wouldn't you *want* your boss to keep a very close eye on what you're doing—at least to start? Most people would.

But if you take this approach as a manager, things can go

wrong very quickly if you haven't clarified what you are up to and why. Otherwise, the risk is that your subordinate will conclude that this is how you'll manage them forever—that "you're a micromanager" rather than "you're helping them get off to a strong start."

But if you've spoken with them about it—and agreed that the amount of autonomy they can expect to get will increase over time, based on clear and objective criteria, then there is no need for them to label you a control freak and no need for you to err on the side of giving them too much rope just so they don't resent you. Instead, you'll have reached an explicit agreement about how you will manage them over time.

The Four Stages of Autonomy

As I mentioned, what's been missing is a simple framework that you and your reports can refer to in order to develop a shared vision of how and how fast they can grow into higher stages of autonomy. I find that this simple four-stage framework—Apprentice ("learning how to do things"), Qualified ("doing things"), Proven ("doing things *and* making sure they are done well"), and Empowered ("knowing what needs to be done")—captures the key points and supports effective dialogue leading to better alignment:

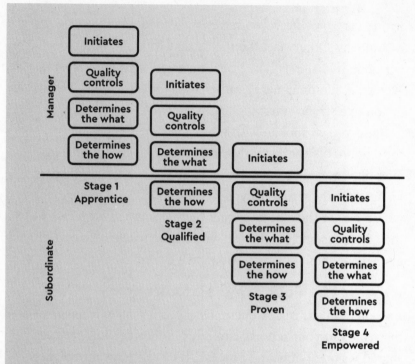

Figure 7.1. The subordinate manager chart, which illustrates the four stages of autonomy.

Stage 1: Apprentice ("Learning How to Do Things")

No matter how smart or experienced your people are, there are always things they'll need to learn almost from scratch—because they lack task-relevant experience. If they can approach these assignments with a beginner's mindset, they're likely to have a much better time of it.

In terms of autonomy, if you're delegating something to someone at this stage, it means you'll be not only telling your subordinate *what* to do, in concrete terms, but also giving them reasonably detailed guidance on *how* they should do it.

In terms of oversight, you'll want to check in with them frequently to see how they're doing, answer questions, offer further guidance, and oversee the quality of their work.

Delegation at the Apprentice Stage

Rhoda, the head of talent acquisition at PicaPica Software, had just hired a new recruiter, Andy. His job was to recruit senior software engineers. While he had done a similar role before, it had been at a bank with a very different culture and recruiting process. So, the two of them agreed that, at the outset, she would keep a close eye on aspects of his work, including how he built his talent pipeline, how he evaluated people, and how he aligned with the hiring manager on who should ultimately get an offer. They also agreed that she would review his draft employment contracts, as PicaPica's contracts were different from the industry standard. She said he could call her at any time to ask questions and mentioned that she'd look over his shoulder once a day or so for the first few weeks. Finally, she explained that this high-touch oversight was only to make sure he got off to a great start, and that assuming all went well, they'd revisit the way they worked together after two months.

Stage 2: Qualified ("Doing Things")

Once someone has proven that they have a basic mastery of the task or process they are charged with handling, it's time to take a step back. At this point, they should be able to do much of the work with less frequent guidance. In particular, you probably no longer need to offer them guidance on *how* they should approach it—either because they already know how or because they can be relied on to figure it out.

You continue to oversee and quality-control their work as it progresses, but your check-ins can be *less frequent*—you might even wait until they are finished before assessing their work. But once it's ready to be assessed, you're still very actively involved in reviewing it, giving them the chance to develop their skills even further as you identify ways in which the work could be improved.

Delegation at the Qualified Stage

After two months, Rhoda and Andy met for their regular one-to-one, but Rhoda allowed for some extra time so that they could discuss how they should adjust the way they'd been working together. She asked him how confident he was in different aspects of his job, and then shared her feedback, which was mostly very complimentary, together with a few pointers.

Rhoda then suggested it was time for them to move up a stage. She still wanted to review the senior candidates that Andy recommended to hiring managers but no longer felt the need to review how he sourced or vetted them. They agreed that he should still feel free to ask her if he had any questions about sourcing or vetting but that otherwise, these were his calls to make.

Rhoda also mentioned that she wouldn't be popping by to see what he was working on anymore. Instead, she'd prefer if he let her know when he had candidates ready to discuss so they could align on candidate quality. She also said that she'd like to continue to review employment agreements before they went out, but only for people at a level 9 or above. Andy was fine with this, as this was the level where nonstandard terms became more common. Although he hadn't felt that her high-touch oversight had been necessary, it hadn't bothered him since she'd been explicit that it was temporary—and today's meeting backed that up.

Stage 3: Proven ("Doing Things and Making Sure They Are Done Well")

The key difference at stage 3 is that you're expecting your

subordinate to produce high-quality work *without you needing to review it*. In other words, they will need to quality-control their own work. This, of course, also implies that they'll need little if any checking up on. Instead, the working assumption is that, if they have doubts or questions, they'll come to you for help.

Delegation at the Proven Stage

Some months later, Rhoda invited Andy out to lunch. At first, they chatted casually; then she introduced her main topic: she felt Andy was ready to go to stage 3 in autonomy on all but director-level searches. She had seen how he had mastered their approach and tuned in to the kinds of people and skills they looked for. She'd also seen him build relationships with his peers and hiring managers and how effectively he dealt with borderline cases. So, they agreed he would start making all the final hiring recommendations himself—and finalize their employment contracts—without her review or oversight.

Rhoda then introduced the other reason for the lunch: she wanted to get Andy's thoughts about whether they should upgrade their talent acquisition system in the coming budget year, and if so, what options to look at.

Stage 4: Empowered ("Knowing What Needs to Be Done")

The first three stages of autonomy all refer to how well your people can deliver the work they're tasked with and with what level of oversight. By stage 3, they can consistently produce great work with minimal oversight from you—which sounds perfect. So, is anything still missing?

It is. In fact, the single most important factor in making your teams more scalable is your people's ability *to know what needs to be done*—and to initiate it. Being empowered is the highest stage of autonomy. In my experience, it's the least well understood but the most important to understand.

> ## The single most important factor in making your teams more scalable is your people's ability *to know what needs to be done*— and to initiate it.

When you're dealing with employees at stages 1 through 3, you're still the one who needs to figure out what needs to be done next. If you're a senior executive, these are the very questions that keep you up at night: What aren't we doing that we should be doing? What might we be overlooking? What's around the corner that we need to worry about? What will my boss expect of me that I haven't already programmed into the work streams?

When all your reports are good, but none is operating at stage 4, the pressure on you to constantly think ahead is intense. But as soon as you have some people who are sharing this burden, then you're really able to fly.

Delegating at the Empowered Stage

Nearly two years had passed, and PicaPica was growing even faster than before, leaving Rhoda's department stretched to the limit. As a result, she and Andy hadn't sat down together for some time. So, when they met for their biannual review, he was curious as to what she would have to say.

Rhoda pulled out a piece of paper with some hand-scrawled notes on it. He couldn't quite read her writing, but he noticed that each point had either an A or an R in a circle next to it— indicating, presumably, Andy or Rhoda.

It turned out that each of those points related to a sugges-tion one of them had made about new projects, initiatives, or approaches they should undertake in their department.

Rhoda's point was that, over the past six months, Andy had contributed nearly half of these suggestions. Andy briefly worried he was going to get a scolding from her for trying to do her job or getting too big for his britches. But, no, Rhoda was delighted, and she wanted to thank him for showing so much ownership and initiative.

This time there was nothing she wanted to change in terms of how she managed him or how they interacted—she just wanted to acknowledge his significant growth and encourage Andy to keep it up. "At this rate, you'll be ready to take on my role soon—and that's exactly what this company needs, given our growth," she said.

Self-Directing People Are the Pillars of Scaling

If you think about the people who have worked for you who truly stood out—the ones who made you privately think, "God I love working with them"—they probably all had this one thing in common: They often knew what needed to be done. They always had their eye on the future, and instead of waiting for you to tell them what needed to be done next, they frequently anticipated it. Then they either went ahead and did it or proposed it to you.

My former executive assistant, Laura, was a master of ini-tiation. I was planning to ask her to design some new pro-cesses that might help us run the business more efficiently—after she'd completed her probationary period. But long before I got that chance, she came to me and suggested four areas in which we needed better processes—two of which

I had been planning to ask her to work on and two I hadn't even thought of!

The number of people who know what needs to be done and can initiate action is the single biggest driver of organizational scalability. The more your people can initiate, the larger your teams can be and the more projects they can take on. And the less you'll be a bottleneck. Plus, initiators are your top candidates for new managerial roles because they're already doing part of your job: thinking ahead. Those people will transition to management roles more successfully than superstar performers who don't initiate.

All this is invaluable in any organization, but it's especially important in high-growth companies, where teams need to be growing and multiplying all the time to scale the business. That's why it's crucial for scaling managers to cultivate the skill of initiation in their employees.

As you can see, it's not enough for you to calibrate the right stage of an employee's autonomy in your mind and choose how to manage them accordingly. Rather, you have to have an ongoing dialogue with them about it. What stage of autonomy do each of you feel is right? Why? What drives that thinking? What needs to be true in your mind before they are ready for the next stage—and what timeline feels doable to both of you for them to achieve that?

My experience is that few managers have discussions of this type, valuable as they are, because they lacked the language or framework to discuss it. The four stages of autonomy should make it easy for you. Nailing this is one of the most powerful levers a manager has in order to increase both Productivity and Positivity. When your management style is fully aligned with your employees' current stages of mastery and their expectations of how they should be managed, then they won't fail or flail as a result of too much autonomy or get demotivated from having too little. Instead, they will be set up for both motivation and success.

As you practice these conversations, you'll soon develop a much better feel for how long different people will take to move up to higher stages of autonomy. This is a crucial step toward knowing how to scale your teams.

Finally, maximizing each employee's stage of autonomy will undoubtedly improve your employee retention. Research shows that people consistently choose gains in autonomy over increased pay or benefits.[4] This is especially important in a start-up, where the opportunities to move up the ladder formally may be more limited than in a large corporation. By helping your employees increase their autonomy—and showing them clearly that it's happening—you can give them a tangible sense of progress in their careers.

Factories That Produce First-Time Managers

These examples show how your manager-employee interactions are a crucial driver of Positivity, Productivity, and scalability. But if you're running a high-growth company, you're busy. The company is doing great things, people are excited, and engagement scores may well be high. In this environment, it's easy to conclude that improving line management is a low priority.

And it's true that when things are going well, employees may be willing to overlook their managers' flaws—they're pumped about the company, and the whole thing feels more like an adventure than a job. But these halcyon periods rarely last long. At some point, things stabilize, or your company hits tougher times. Then, when the adrenaline wears off, your people will

---

[4] See Holger Reisinger and Dane Fetterer, "Forget Flexibility. Your Employees Want Autonomy," *Harvard Business Review*, October, 29 2021, hbr.org/2021/10/forget-flexibility-your-employees-want-autonomy.

realize that their job is . . . a job. At that point, if their manager sucks, it's a real problem.

Or perhaps you feel your current crop of managers are doing a pretty good job despite your not having invested in them. If they are, it's probably down to luck, and there's not much chance your luck will hold as the company grows and the number of managers multiplies. Why? Because any fast-growing business is a factory for producing first-time managers. As your head count grows, you'll inevitably promote a lot of your best individual contributors into their first management roles. That's the right thing to do given their knowledge of the business, as well as for their own career development. But having lots of managers with no management experience *and little or no training* is a recipe for future problems.

If you overlook the crucial step of building great line managers early on, it comes back to bite you. The best managers will be able to retain top talent, produce impressive results, and keep morale high, while the worst will drive valuable people away, create internal friction, and slow the company down. I encourage you to make effective line management a foundational pillar of your scaling strategy. If you invest in this early on, it will free up time down the road, as your organization will have far more scalability and far fewer people issues. Now is the best possible time to get started.

The best managers will be able to retain top talent, produce impressive results, and keep morale high, while the worst will drive valuable people away, create internal friction, and slow the company down.

Ritual 4:
Effective Delegation and Aligning on Autonomy

This is a straightforward ritual designed to ensure that when you delegate something, you set your subordinate up for success. It comes in two parts: a preparation guide and a discussion guide. Next time you are about to ask one of your team to take on a new piece of work, take a few minutes to answer the following questions before you meet them.

Preparation Guide for Managers in Advance of Delegating a Task, Project, or Process

- **Define the task and the outcome.**

  - What is the task or project I am planning to delegate?

  - What is the context for this piece of work? Why is it important? Why has it arisen now?

  - Where and how does this fit in to the rest of the team's/this person's work?

  - What is the main outcome that must be achieved?

  - How will this outcome be measured?

  - What does good look like?

- **Prioritize.**

  - What other outcomes are important (if any)? How will these be measured?

  - When must this task be completed by? Why? Are there key milestones along the way? (Or, if it's an ongoing process, what are the key milestones?)

  - How important is this task relative to other demands on the person's time?

- **Resource.**

  - What type of support or input should they expect to get
    from me? How can they best use me?

  - What other people or resources are they likely to need to draw on? What constraints should they be aware of in using these resources?

- **Establish an appropriate stage of autonomy.**

  - What is their task-relevant experience? Where do I think they are in terms of the four stages of autonomy?

  - Based on this, what stage of autonomy am I planning to give them in terms of defining how the work gets done? How closely will I monitor their approaches, and what will I be looking for?

  - What stage of autonomy am I going to give them in terms of quality-controlling their work? What will my oversight be focused on?

  - Overall, how frequently do I expect to interact with them on this piece of work? Who should initiate those interactions?

Discussion Guide

Once you've shared this context, here are some discussion questions for when you meet with your team member:

- Is there anything that needs further clarification?

- How confident are you that you can achieve the targets, deadlines, etc.?

- What do you see as the biggest obstacles or risks?

- How comfortable are you with the support and resources at your disposal? Is there anything else you feel you will need?

- Does the stage of autonomy I am proposing here feel appropriate? Is it consistent with the overall "journey to autonomy" we have previously mapped out?

- What else would help us to be fully aligned on this?

Managers Are Also Coaches

As a manager, a core part of your job is to help your people become more effective and more autonomous—to find their own solutions to the challenges they face. This is done through coaching. By asking questions instead of giving solutions, you encourage your team members to think more deeply about their tasks and challenges. When they are able to find their own solutions—even in part—then that is valuable learning for them. They'll also be more committed to following through than when the solutions come entirely from you, so by coaching them, you can boost both their Productivity and Positivity, as well as support their professional development.

Coaching is most effective when it's focused on an issue where *they* feel stuck. This could either be an "it" issue—some technical or business challenge—or an "us" issue—perhaps an interpersonal challenge they're having with a customer, vendor, or colleague. So, you'll want to kick off any coaching discussions by finding out what their pain points are. You may have other areas that you need them to address or improve at, and that's where the following feedback ritual comes in.

Ritual 5:
Coaching a Pain Point

There are many good guides for how to be an effective manager and coach, and many good coaching questions, so please treat these as examples. What's key is how you listen: after asking a question, compose yourself to listen calmly and patiently, with the same curious energy you learned in the Thinking Together Ritual (page 55).

Coaching should be a core part of your regular one-to-ones, but you can also coach someone spontaneously anytime you have a few minutes together. Here are some good questions to ask:

- What are you finding most challenging in your work right now?
- What's making this hard for you?
- What does success look like?
- Why is this important for you?
- How might you be getting in your own way?
- What are you afraid of?
- What would you do if you were not afraid?
- What is the real challenge for you?
- What is your intuition telling you?
- What do you know now that you didn't know earlier?

Try to avoid offering your opinion as you listen to their answers. I know it's hard. But here's a very simple and powerful guideline, courtesy of Nancy Kline from her book *Time to Think: Listening to Ignite the Human Mind*: you can have the benefit of my thinking—once you've taken your own thinking as far as it can go."

Once you're convinced that, through the quality of your questions and your listening, your team member has taken their thinking as far as it can go—then ask yourself if that's good enough for now, or if you'll actually be holding them back by not offering them your own thinking. If so, add this final question to your coaching conversation: "Would you like to hear my thoughts on this issue, or do you feel you have all you need?"

They'll almost certainly want to hear your views—but on the odd chance they say something like "No, thanks, I'm actually completely clear on what I need to do," you'll probably do more harm than good by speaking up! Sit back, and watch them roll.

Breaking the Feedback Logjam

Giving feedback is another area where many managers struggle. There are thousands of books, blogs, and YouTube videos on how to give great feedback—yet with all this help out there, why is it that so many managers still struggle to give valuable feedback?

We learned the answer in chapter 7: our AI filters kick in and keep us from speaking openly, unless we have a sufficiently high level of trust. I saw this in Justin, the conflict-avoidant CEO of an SaaS company. Because he couldn't give tough feedback, two of his executives were allowed to underperform for far too long. Everyone knew it was a problem . . . except these two. When their underperformance came under the spotlight in a workshop, it was much more painful than it would have been if the CEO had been able to surface the problem much earlier. Ritual 6 will help you break the feed-back logjam by giving honest feedback.

Ritual 6:
Contracting for Feedback

Giving honest feedback can be difficult, but this ritual will make it easier. It's normal and healthy to be concerned about how your words might have made the other person feel. Few of us *enjoy* having our weaknesses called out—but that doesn't mean we don't need the feedback in order to grow. As a manager, if you hold back from sharing feedback, you're really just protecting yourself from those awkward feelings—but you're depriving your employee of a necessary chance to learn and develop. These three tips should get you going in the right direction—and keep in mind that the more you do it, the easier it becomes.

Practice having "us" conversations before you need to offer any tough love. This starts with sharing your PUGs (page 97), then building on that to have discussions about how the two of you can work better together on other "us" topics that you do feel comfortable surfacing. Ask them to let you know what they want to improve on or what they would value your feedback on. This also comes out of their PUG, but it may change quite often, so I would encourage you to ask this question every two to three months. Once they've explicitly asked you for your feedback, it's a whole lot easier to share it without your AI filter stopping you.

Contract for feedback. This is a particularly powerful hack. If you struggle with being direct or sharing difficult feedback, let your employee know this and *ask for their express permission to be direct with them.* You can contract with them for feedback in general or on a particular topic. For example, you might say, "June, we've discussed your need to be more concise and not ramble on in team meetings, but I find it hard to point out when you could have done better, as I'm worried it'll discourage or upset you. Are you really open to hearing this feedback whenever I see an opportunity for you to have done better?" Or, "June, I think you know I find it quite hard to be direct with people, as I worry I'll upset them, so I wanted to ask if my being candid and direct—perhaps even a little blunt when necessary—is okay with you?"

Once you have heard them say, "Yes, 100 percent, I want you to be up front with me about this" or something similar, it's much easier for you to speak openly, even if you normally tend to avoid conflict. And here's what's particularly interesting: almost everyone you put this question to will say they want your feedback straight up!

Do plenty of listening when you give feedback. Feedback sessions should not be one-way conversations. Your team member may have all kinds of things to say in response to the feedback you've shared—and their range of reactions is too broad to deal with all possible scenarios here. But the essential point is to make sure that you're listening to what they say—even if you don't agree with it—and that they feel heard.

Appreciation Ain't Thanks

Research into employee satisfaction consistently shows that being appreciated is a major factor. The problem is that most managers say things like "Thanks for staying up late to finish this project." That's showing appreciation for something specific the person did, which is not a bad thing. But it's transactional. Someone does something for you; you say thank you. There typically isn't much thought behind it, and after a while, it can start to feel empty. The employee thinks, "I have to stay up late to hit these deadlines all the time, and all I get is a quick thank-you, like it's no big deal."

On the other hand, when you appreciate people for *who they are* instead of what they've done, it makes them feel seen and appreciated on a deeper level. In this case, it might sound like this: "Hey, Tom, I just wanted to say that I notice whenever we have tough deadlines, you're always the one volunteering to stay up late to finish things. I just wanted to say that I really respect and appreciate that about you."

This shows that you value them as people and care about your relationship with them. This is a powerful way to build trust and goodwill that most managers never use.

Ritual 7:
The Complete One-to-Ones

Regular one-to-ones between managers and their reports are the essential building block of effective line management. But because a one-to-one can cover such a range of topics, I won't try to prescribe every element. Instead, I'll share an outline that encompasses the core elements of effective one-to-ones, including the rituals we have just learned.

Step 1: Check in. How are they doing? If you're aware of any issues in their health, with their family, or anything else, now's a good time to ask about it, if appropriate.

Step 2: Find their pain points, and coach them on them. Before you get into topics you want to focus on, start with a topic or two that they want to focus on. Use the Coaching a Pain Point Ritual (page 128) at this point in your one-to-one.

Step 3: Share mutual feedback. Hopefully by now you've built a high-trust relationship and/or contracted for feedback (page 130), so you won't find it so hard to share your thoughts. Remember that tough feedback only gets harder to give the longer you wait.

Now is also the right time to ask them for their feedback on what you can do better or differently. Make sure they know that speaking up in this way isn't a problem—it's an essential part of achieving high performance. This is also the right time to check in on your working relationship. You can ask questions like:

- What is working well in our current setup, and what could be improved?
- How could we collaborate better?
- What are your thoughts on our communication and workflow?

Step 4: Delegate any new tasks. Use the Effective Delegation and Aligning on Autonomy Ritual (page 125) to do so.

Step 5: Check in on autonomy. From time to time, discuss how much autonomy they currently have, how well they're coping with it, and what each of you would expect or hope for. Encourage them to develop their self-directing muscle by always asking, "What else needs to be done?"

Step 6: Cover their agenda. Give them the opportunity to ask questions, raise red flags, or bring up anything else that might be on their mind. If they do ask for help with a problem, avoid the temptation to simply solve it for them. Instead, consider the coaching approach again.

Step 7: Share appreciation. Try to end the conversation by sharing something you've picked up about them during this conversation that you appreciated. Perhaps they showed a real openness to hearing feedback, an eagerness to learn new skills, a willingness to take on extra work to cover for an absent employee, or a high degree of creativity in their approach to problem-solving—all of these are likely to be positive character traits as opposed to one-off behaviors, and they're worth commending the person on. So you might say, "I really appreciate how creative you are in thinking up solutions to these kinds of problems," or "I appreciate the way you support your team members."

Recap

- Nothing drives Productivity and Positivity in your organization more than the quality of your line managers.

- High-growth companies naturally produce a lot of first-time managers who often lack the skills they need to be effective.

- Investing in training your managers early pays off, as it helps you generate results, retain top talent, develop your people, and maintain high morale.

- Managers should always encourage their reports to stretch themselves toward higher levels of autonomy— while at the same time being up front with them about the stage of autonomy they are currently comfortable granting.

- Coaching is a core skill for managers that helps employees grow and become more autonomous.

- It's crucial that managers provide candid feedback, but many struggle. Contracting for Feedback is a powerful ritual that can help.

- Holding regular one-to-ones that include the core elements of delegation, coaching, feedback, and appreciation is the foundation of effective line management.

Chapter 8

Top Team Building Rituals

▾

This chapter demonstrates the critical role that a unified and aligned top team plays in building a high-performing, friction-free organization.

WE'VE SEEN HOW COMPLEXITY can overtake a company, resulting in organizational friction that can slow you down. In a smaller organization, a CEO who is good at orchestration can manage much of the complexity themselves, integrating all the threads of activity and addressing issues as they arise—but this runs out of runway soon enough, since complexity grows exponentially.

But CEOs are not the only bottlenecks to successful scaling. In this chapter, we'll learn how your top team can compound organizational friction—or be a powerful antidote. This chapter goes hand in hand with the following one, in which we explore why having executives who are truly operating at the C-suite level (often referred to as CXOs), rather than relying on departmental or functional heads, is essential for scaling, and what the difference is between a CXO and a functional head.

In this chapter, we'll learn what it takes for teams to operate at high levels of Productivity and Positivity and how vital that is for the rest of the organization. But first, let's look at the role of the CEO in building a unifying—rather than a fragmenting—top team.

Leading for Expediency

If you're a CEO, you have a choice about how much to engage your senior executives on issues beyond the immediate scope of their functional roles. It's a spectrum, but let's explore the edges of the spectrum: the bilateral and the collective approach.

Pavel is the CEO of Token Trade, an amazingly successful cryptocurrency decacorn. He has a touch of business genius in him, but he's also a strong introvert who dislikes working in groups. As a result, he tries to work bilaterally whenever possible—meaning he tackles marketing issues with the CMO, technology issues with the CTO, and so on. He's okay to pull in a third person but will resist setting meetings with more than three, even when that's logical. Apart from quick update calls, the full executive team only meets for deeper discussions once or twice per year.

Pavel likes the bilateral approach because it *feels* fast since, of course, two people can come to an agreement on an issue more quickly than six. As a result, his schedule is full of these relatively simple interactions that don't require a lot of advance thought, preparation, or group facilitation skills on his part and that allow him to get in and out quickly.

Leading for Collective Action

Jin, the CEO of a dating app called DataDate, is the opposite of Pavel. He prefers to get his top team to work collectively on any big strategic, commercial, or organizational issue, even if not everyone strictly needs to be there. Not all these meetings are equally productive, and in total, they take up a considerable amount of executive time. On the face of it, Pavel's leadership model seems far more efficient. But is it?

The problem with Pavel's bilateral model is that it tends toward *fragmentation*: different leadership team members having different interpretations of the strategy. Or different takes on the most urgent priorities. Or different understandings of what customers really care about. Or inconsistent views about who is responsible for what and where the boundaries between departments and functions are drawn. And so on.

Think of Pavel as a laser that emits a pure, coherent light. This light carries all kinds of important information on topics including vision, strategy, priorities, roles and responsibilities, the implications of key policies and decisions, and so on. (Of course, many CEOs are far from coherent in their thinking and communications—which leads to even greater complexity—but let's assume you have a coherent CEO for now.)

As Pavel works bilaterally with his executives, each gets exposed to different aspects of his thinking. The context in which the issues come up is inevitably different, causing the emphasis or level of detail to change. On top of that, they will of course interpret what he says in their own way—and Pavel admits that he often "fine-tunes" what he says to make it more palatable to whichever executive he's speaking with. As a result, each executive walks away satisfied that they have reached a common understanding and that Pavel was responsive to any points or concerns they raised. Pavel feels good about it, too, because each of these conversations is fast and ends on a positive note. But each of these conversations effectively refracts Pavel's coherent vision in a different way, like a prism bending light.

As these executives return to their departments and engage their teams, they inevitably put their own spin on what they've discussed with Pavel, resulting in further refraction. Soon there is a multitude of interpretations. As the light passes through more people, it's as if it hits not only a prism but also a disco ball, creating a huge range of colors and patterns that are constantly shifting.

Over time, this leads to misunderstandings and conflicts, which lead to mistrust, silos, hoarding of information, interpersonal conflict, blaming, and other collaboration barriers.

The fragmentation resulting from Pavel's style of leadership ultimately slows his organization down. Jin's collective approach takes lots of CXO time—but since his CXOs have competent departmental heads who can run the day-to-day, it doesn't slow things down—in fact, the alignment they build allows the rest of the organization to speed up.

The reason many CEOs stick with the binary approach is that *they're not the ones who experience the negative effects.* Their meetings all feel sharp, focused, and efficient. Their executives all walk out of their office happy and clear on what's next. It's further down in the organization that these misalignments play out, leading to conflict, poor collaboration, duplication of work, gaps in processes, and other dysfunctions and inefficiencies.

The reason many CEOs stick with the binary approach is that they're not the ones who experience the negative effects. Their meetings all feel sharp, focused, and efficient.

When they are alerted to this problem, bilateral CEOs tend to say, "These people just need to figure out how to work together." They think they can push the responsibility for fixing these issues down to lower levels. But they're wrong.

Which Team Comes First?

It's not just bilateral CEOs who resist the collective approach. It's common for CXOs and functional heads to view the top team as their second priority, so conflicts at that level don't bother them that much. Instead, they focus their energies on building clarity and alignment within the team that reports to them. These executives still believe that they're driven by what's best for the company as a whole, but this mindset almost always leads to them taking their team's point of view over the company's at key junctures.

Few people have made this point more powerfully than Patrick Lencioni. As he explains in *The Five Dysfunctions of a Team*, his seminal 2002 book, when senior executives prioritize their departments' needs and perspectives over those of the company as a whole, it leads to frictions and inefficiencies lower down in the organization. He believes that the more constructive conflict there is within the top team—ultimately leading to true alignment—the less destructive conflict there is in the rest of the organization.

Leading for Scalability

It's not just Jin's approach that's different; it's also his mindset. He doesn't see himself as being the sole person responsible for shining the light that guides his company. He's happy to take executive decisions from time to time, but he sees his role more as bringing out others' ideas, as well as his own, and guiding the team to reach deep alignment.

Jin's process definitely takes more time, both for him and his executives. But instead of fragmentation, it leads to *cohesion*. Now, instead of the eight people on his leadership team conveying messages of slightly different meaning and emphasis, he has eight executives shining the same light across all parts of the organization. Diffraction and diffusion will still take place, but at a much lower level and with much less loss of fidelity.

CEOs who try this without first mastering a few skills may well find that they lose some of the speed and decisiveness they had early on. This can easily lead them to conclude that being more inclusive and harnessing the benefits of the full team are incompatible with being fast and decisive. But with a bit of practice, this is soon a false trade-off.

Running a more collective and inclusive leadership model has several other important advantages:

- By participating in these discussions, your executives will develop a deeper understanding of the context for, and intent of, decisions, as well as feel more committed to them. These both lead to better execution.

- Executives who might start out with narrow functional expertise get exposed to a wide range of issues, which prepares them to take on broader management roles in the future.

- CEOs also benefit: they get much more insight into the leadership skills of their team members, rather than seeing them purely through the lens of their functional skills.

- Finally, it's a powerful recruiting tool—executives have a choice about where to work, and they may very well choose your company over an alternative if they know they'll have a seat at the table when you are taking the key decisions.

When you're small, both the bilateral and the collective approach work well. But the larger your organization is, the less effective bilateral leadership will be. What seems fast to you will bog down the rest of your organization. Building a collective leadership team takes time and skill, but in a scaling organization, it pays off tenfold. As the African proverb says, "If you want to run fast, run alone. If you want to run far, run together."

Ritual 8:
Deep-Dive Meetings

Nothing drives team performance up—or down—more than the quality of its deep-dive meetings—the ones where the big strategic, commercial, operational, and organizational decisions are made. These are also the meetings where the cohesion of the team is forged and where you transform your top executives from being a source of fragmentation and friction lower down the organization into a source of coherence that reduces friction. If you master the art of running brilliant deep-dive meetings, you'll be well on your way to peak performance.

Step 1: Plan in advance. A little advance planning goes a huge way toward making your deep-dive meetings more impactful and efficient. There are four things to do before the meeting starts:

- Determine the *most important issues* for your team to focus on right now. So much invaluable time is wasted going through updates or addressing necessary but low-value issues. Set your agenda so that the key strategic, commercial, or operational issues are tackled *first*.

- Define the *outcome* you want from each agenda item. Is it a list of options? A decision? A detailed action plan to kick off a new project?

- Ensure that everyone has the critical information they need to engage effectively with the issue—ideally in memo form. This can be distributed in advance or read together in the meeting. Avoid presentations of more than ten slides during the meeting itself.

Step 2: Set up for success. Now you're in the meeting itself. A few things will really help get everyone in the right frame of mind:

- Ask everyone to switch off any devices or apps that are likely to distract them and to give their full attention to the discussion.

- Don't dive straight in. Too often people rush to meetings distracted by thoughts of the previous meeting or stressed out by the pressures of the day. That's no way to get into a great discussion. Instead, open the meeting with a warm-up round, using a mindset-shifting question like, "What's going well for you at work right now?" Even better, ask everyone to close their eyes and take five deep breaths. It takes thirty seconds, which even the hardest-core business types can deal with it. They may roll their eyes, but they'll notice how much more focus there is in the room just moments later.

Step 3: Align on the question.[5] Make sure you're all fully agreed on the specific question that needs to be answered today. Too often, team meetings have vague agenda items like "sales" or "financials." Everyone has something to say about these topics, but no one is clear on what specific question you're trying to answer, so they're not focused on the same issue. As a result, people end up talking past each other. Or they discuss questions that are important but that can't be answered today. A good question does the following:

- Highlights where you're stuck, the problem at hand (e.g., falling sales this quarter).

- Defines the outcome you hope to achieve in today's meeting (e.g., a list of possible actions to reverse the trend).

Once you've clarified the question, read the energy in the room. If it's high and people are eager to dive in, you're on the right question.

Step 4: Hold a round. In any group, there are some people who take up a lot of airtime and others who take up very little. One might be the most senior person in the room as well as an outgoing, confident extrovert from a culture that values speaking up, and they are speaking their native language. Another may be a quiet introvert, relatively junior or new compared to others in the room, a non-native speaker, or someone from a culture that values deference to seniority.

The thing is, these factors have no correlation with how valuable their respective contributions might be. To really get

---

[5] Steps 3 and 4 are drawn from the work of one of my most influential teachers, Nancy Kline. I strongly recommend that you read her book *Time to Think: Listening to Ignite the Human Mind* to get a deeper understanding of her philosophy and the powerful techniques she has developed.

the collective-thinking engine going, you have to give everyone the space to share their best ideas. This is where the round comes in. Restate the question you arrived at in step 3; then kick off the round. Here are the rules:

- Anyone can start. Go around clockwise or counterclockwise until everyone has spoken.

- Listeners should pay full attention to the speaker. Keep your eyes on them while they're speaking. And focus on understanding the meaning of their message, not on what you want to say in response. You'll get your turn in a minute.

- Under no circumstances should you interrupt or jump in. Even if you desperately want to ask a clarifying question or make a point—hold it! Instead, write it down so you don't lose it. (The risk if you do break the round is that someone responds to you, and then you to them, and soon the round has collapsed, and you're back having a debate between the two or three loudest voices.)

Rounds are dead simple, but I can't count the number of times I've seen them transform a team. That's because a round is more than a mechanical device. It's also a *powerful social contract* that both binds and liberates the people in the meeting. This is the implicit contract. As a member of this team:

- I know *categorically* that I will have a chance to speak to our biggest issues.

- I know that when I speak, I will not be interrupted and that others will be 100 percent focused on listening to me. I know I'll be heard and have a chance to influence others.

- In exchange for this privilege, I will keep my remarks

concise—and will give others my fullest attention when it's their turn to speak.

Step 5: Use a talking stick. Once your opening round is finished, you're all free to jump in and discuss the issues as you normally would, with one small change: use a talking stick. It's simple—only the person holding the talking stick (a marker pen works perfectly) is allowed to speak. (You can achieve the same thing in virtual meetings using the mute button.)

Simple as this is, it's incredibly powerful because it eliminates the possibility of interruptions. When people know for sure that they won't be interrupted, a huge amount of stress and pressure disappears. They can choose their words with care and pause, and they can think while they speak without worrying that someone will steal the floor from them. As a result, the quality of contributions skyrockets, and the number of misunderstandings plummets.

Keep an eye on equality of participation. If two or three people are dominating the discussion, invite the others to say how they see things. Or you can hold another round to ask people what their *latest* thinking is, in light of what has been said so far. This is often enough to find that the group is ready to move toward a conclusion or decision—and if not, it highlights exactly where any outstanding issues still lie, enabling you to focus on those points.

Step 6: Check Productivity and Positivity. If you feel that things aren't going well but you're not sure why, refer to your Productivity and Positivity matrix (page 62) and ask people which quadrant they're in. If you're stuck in the Comforting quadrant, ask someone to make a clear proposal to move the group toward an answer. If you're in the Intimidating quadrant, holding a latest thinking round will calm the room and ensure everyone feels heard.

It may seem like there's a lot to this ritual, but it's pretty simple when you step back and look at the big picture. To have a great deep-dive meeting, you need to have the right people in the room, be clear on the question you're there to answer, hear and consider every perspective, and pursue shared understanding until the team comes to a conclusion everyone can commit to. By using the Productivity and Positivity matrix, you can keep the meeting on track. Most teams get amazing results very quickly, but it does require some skillful facilitation.

Will You Get Anything Done This Way?

You may think I'm proposing a world of consensus, where no boss steps in to speed up the decision-making process. I'm not. In fact, I'm a huge fan of leaders who drive conversations to make them Productive, Positive, *and time efficient*. The problem is that not enough leaders know how to do this.

Picture a meeting in which everyone shares their perspective, then the leader makes a decision based on what they've heard. Most leaders are very good at this. When an issue is a simple choice, such as "Should we launch our international expansion this year or next year?" then this approach works well enough. But the reality is that few decisions are as simple as this. There are compelling reasons to expand this year (to gain a first-mover advantage) and good reasons to wait (you can't afford it). The question that would be better here is "How can we capture a significant first-mover advantage internationally while living within this year's financial constraints?" That requires the skill of collective thinking first—and then a decision.

Interestingly, the word *decide* is derived from a Latin word meaning "to cut or kill." It's the same root you find in words such as *homicide, suicide,* and *pesticide.* To ask a leader to "decide" is to ask them to kill off some alternatives in order to choose one. And that's a good and necessary thing. But it's a different process—and a different skill—from asking them to "generate better alternatives." One process kills ideas; the other gives birth to new ones.

Capable leaders should be equally adept at both.

Ritual 9:
Coach Your Team from the Balcony

When Productivity or Positivity aren't as high as you'd like them to be, you'll want to know why and what you can do about it. This ritual will give you the tool you need to figure that out.

Imagine that your business discussions take place on a dance floor. Overlooking the dance floor is a balcony.[6] From there, you can all see and discuss your behaviors as a team.

The balcony is a safe place. It's a place where you park your discussions and differences on the topic at hand in order to focus on the quality of the discussion / meeting and what would make it better.

Start by asking everyone where they are on the Productivity and Positivity matrix. If most people are in the Comforting quadrant, that may indicate that people are being overly polite and are tiptoeing around what they really think. You can ask people if that's the case, and if so, what's holding them back. Once you're done with that discussion, you can return

---

[6] This idea was developed by Ron Heifetz in his book *The Practice of Adaptive Leadership.*

to the dance floor and ask who has a clear proposal that would move the discussion forward.

If some people are in the Frustrating or Intimidating quadrants, that means they're not entirely comfortable with the way the discussion is being held. Perhaps they found it hard to get a word in, were cut off, or found someone's remarks overly critical. Gently encourage people to share if they were not comfortable, why, and what would make it more comfortable for them.

To keep the balcony a safe environment, remind the group to focus their comments on observable behaviors: who is talking and who isn't, what's being discussed and what isn't, whether people are on their devices, and so on. People should be honest about their observations but avoid blaming statements or making anyone "wrong."

Here are some other questions that support effective balcony discussions:

- What would make this discussion more Productive? How can we do better next time?

- Are we making good use of our time here? If not, how can we speed things up?

- Do you have any specific requests for this group that would make this more comfortable for you?

- Are there any elephants in the room that need to be addressed?

If you're facilitating a balcony discussion, one thing to watch out for is "falling off the balcony," someone introducing a comment that takes the team back to the *content* of the previous discussion rather than the *quality* of the discussion itself. For example, someone might say, "I felt the meeting was going great until Brad said that we should shift our focus to the smaller customers. That's just taking us down the wrong path completely, and I lost my patience at that point." That comment is likely to lead Brad (or someone else) to jump back to the dance floor and say, "No, it actually makes perfect sense, and here's why . . . " If this happens, just note the nature of the comment and ask the person to hold it until the balcony discussion is finished and the team has agreed to go back down to the dance floor.

The more complex your business becomes, the more it will rely on teams to get things done—true teams that actually work *together*, not just as groups of individuals. That's why it's crucial that you and your executives are role models when it comes to running efficient, effective team meetings that build unified teams.

What's amazing about these rituals is that they make a huge difference *immediately*. You don't have to practice them for weeks or months to understand their value. The very first time, you'll see how they increase engagement, boost creativity, lead to better decisions and greater commitment, and build trust. With practice, they'll also save you time. It might feel like a big shift in how you do things, but after a while, you'll wonder how you ever functioned any other way.

The true power of these top team building rituals will become clear as they spread to the rest of the teams in your organization. Just imagine all the valuable ideas that will come out of the woodwork—and how motivated people will be—when everyone has an opportunity to speak up and be heard. Imagine how many problems will be avoided when teams regularly take the time to tune up their ways of working together and work through any frictions.

Let's revisit the working definition of Productivity when applied to a leadership team meeting:

- **Did you work on your most important issues?**

- **Did you harness the collective intelligence of the team to generate ideas, solutions, and decisions better than any one person could have?**

- **Did you build a shared commitment to a clear course of action?**

- **Did you make good progress given the time spent?**

In summary, if you're achieving all of the above, then your team is accomplishing great things. And if you're consistently in the Positive zone, then the trust within the team will be consistently growing, even when it handles challenging issues—which in turn enables the team to perform even better in the future. To me, there is no better definition of a high-performing team than one that consistently accomplishes great things while deepening trust. When all your top teams are operating at that level, you're well on your way to building a scalable, high-performance organization.

Recap

- CEOs often find it expedient to work bilaterally with their senior executives rather than tackling major issues collectively with their top team. The bilateral approach is fine for certain issues, but it leads to fragmentation and different interpretations of strategy and priorities.

- Working collectively takes a bit more time—especially at first until you've gotten the hang of it. But it creates much more cohesion at the top team level and much greater alignment throughout the rest of organization. The result is better, faster execution.

- Ultimately, bilateral leadership can slow down an organization, and collective leadership speeds it up.

- CXOs often prioritize their own teams over the top team, creating tension and potential conflicts of interest. A collective approach to leadership will help them take the company-wide point of view.

- Effective deep-dive meetings are the key building blocks for creating high-performance teams.

- If your team can consistently generate high-Productivity/high-Positivity discussions as it tackles its most important challenges, then by definition it's a high-performing team.

- Teams can learn to coach themselves back on track by mastering the art of going to the balcony.

Chapter 9

Leadership Building Rituals

▼

In this chapter, you'll learn the difference between a department head and a true CXO, why CXOs are essential to building true scalability, and how you can help your top leaders keep pace with the increasingly complex demands of their growing roles.

I F YOU RUN A RELATIVELY SMALL ORGANIZATION, your functional leaders may have a range of titles: "head of" or "VP" or "CXO"—but the truth is that the nature of their jobs doesn't vary much. At this stage, their role, regardless of title, is clear enough: build and run their department effectively. To get the job done and keep their people happy and growing. That typically takes 80 to 90 percent of their time, with the rest spent on cross-functional processes or company-wide initiatives.

But as your organization scales—and for the collective leadership model to work—you're going to need true CXOs, not just functional heads. I'm often struck by how unclear the distinction between the two is to most leaders, even HR directors. So first let's look at the key differences and then figure out how to get your people from here to there.

What CXOs Do

For someone to fulfill the full responsibilities of a CXO, the job of running their department day-to-day should take no more than 50 to 60 percent of their time. For that to work, they'll need competent senior managers who can build teams, run day-to-day operations, and solve problems as they arise. That obviously takes time to develop. So, if you see that your functional heads will need to strengthen their teams considerably to elevate their own roles, then step 2 in the Future-Proof Your CXOs Ritual (page 159) will be crucial.

Once that team is starting to take shape, they'll be able to spend the balance of their time on three other roles that are crucial to the success of a scaling organization: enabling cross-functional collaboration, contributing to top-level decision-making and planning, and reinventing their function. Let's take a closer look at each.

Enabling Cross-Functional Collaboration

As the size of individual departments grows, the number of cross-functional interactions—and the chance for these to become sources of friction—grow exponentially. It's no longer possible to grease the wheels of these interactions one at a time. To make this work, CXOs need to spend a big chunk of their time laying down better tracks for these interactions: building the strategic and operating plans together with their counterparts, developing and refining the joint processes, and deepening the relationships that enable these plans to come to fruition without cross-departmental frictions building up.

Contributing to Top-Level Decision-Making and Planning

In a Day Zero organization, it's easy for the CEO to know pretty much all they need to make key decisions. Not anymore. In a much larger and more complex organization, the range of activities that require the full participation of the CXOs grows to include setting strategy; setting budgets and manpower plans; making major commercial, operational, and organizational decisions; refining the operating rhythm; and more.

This is a big shift in focus and skills for someone whose primary focus until now has been on their department, and the need to make that shift often comes fast. But managers don't always grow as fast as their evolving roles demand, which makes this a challenging time for every functional leader.

Reinventing Their Function

A department of 50 or 150 people is not only a bigger version of what it was when it had 20 people. It's a fundamentally different animal; and it needs different leadership skills, role definitions, business processes, and tools. It also has a vastly more complex internal organization. To lead a department through this journey, a CXO has to take a big step back from the day-to-day pressures of getting stuff done in order to think much longer term about what the future shape of their function should be, how it should operate, and what the steps are to get there.

The Layering Problem

If you're scaling fast, there's little doubt that at some point your company will need a group of true CXOs who can rise above the day-to-day job of running departments. Of course, in an ideal world, your existing functional managers would all grow into that job. But what if they haven't, at least not yet? If you stick with them even after it's clear that they're not going to successfully make the transition, you risk slow-ing your company down and frustrating the best talent below them. But if you hire CXOs from outside and place them above your existing functional leaders (thereby layering the previous departmental heads), you risk losing your old-timers, their institutional knowledge, and the followers who are loyal to them. This is a painful and confusing dilemma for many CEOs.

If you're faced with this dilemma, you might naturally err on the side of being loyal to your existing leaders: after all, they're the ones who have worked so hard for so many years to get your company where it is today. It would seem almost cruel to reward them for the company's success by letting them know that they will no longer report to you. But if you do nothing, some of your leaders will become proverbial boiled frogs: slowly overwhelmed by the increasing complexity of their roles until they're dead in the water. Eventually, the sit-uation becomes unstable, but it doesn't have to be this way.

The problem is that most CEOs start work on this far too late. They can see the water getting hotter around their direct reports, but they don't know how to start the conversation—a perfect example of a critical "us" issue that gets kicked down the road. But once you see the inevitability of this scaling dilemma, it makes perfect sense for you to discuss it with your functional heads *early on*. By working together well before the issue reaches a critical juncture, you should be able to generate two much better scenarios: one in which you help them into the full CXO shoes and another in which you hire an outside executive and have them *be happy* about it. Why? Because over the course of the one to three years the discus-sion has been happening, and through the use of the following ritual, they've become clear on what it actually means to be a CXO, where their gaps are, and how they can accelerate their learning by working closely with someone who has already mastered those skills.

Ritual 10:
Future-Proof Your CXOs

As we've seen, the role of a functional head in a smallish enterprise is very different from the role of a CXO in a larger one. By surfacing and discussing this difference, and coaching your leaders on the gaps you foresee, you give your organization the best chance of scaling smoothly without disruptive changes in leadership—and you give your current leaders the feedback and support they need for long-term success.

Step 1: Have the conversation regularly. You should discuss the difference between your department heads' current role as a leader of their function and the company's future requirements for a true CXO multiple times over the course of their tenure. Ideally, the discussion starts when they first take on their departmental leadership role or when you hire them. This is the best time to communicate your philosophy that everyone—including you—should be prepared to step aside or be layered if they can't keep up with the evolving demands of their role as the company grows. This helps to set their expectations early. It also gives them the most time to develop the capabilities they'll need.

Step 2: Have them create an organizational road map for their function. Work with them to imagine how their function will need to evolve and what it might look like two to three years out. What new capabilities will need to be added? How will the department's current ways of working need to change? Who will they need to hire, and what management structure will be most appropriate? How will their own role need to evolve? Then help them think through how they should go about creating that and how their role should evolve as it happens.

As the two of you work on this, you're picking up invaluable data. The quality of their thinking on these issues provides strong clues as to their potential to keep up with the changing demands of the CXO role.

Step 3: Make a CXO growth plan. Delve into that last question about the evolution of their role, and jointly develop a list of the competencies they'll need to be successful in the CXO role down the road. The challenge for many CEOs is articulating what these are, perhaps because they themselves have never led a company that has reached that next level of scale. They're things you may feel but struggle to put words to. But it's hard to coach someone toward a goal that you can't describe in any detail, so it's important that you invest time in this discussion over a number of sessions. You may also want to engage an executive coach to assist with this.

Step 4: Give feedback and coach. As the two of you get clearer on the future role and competencies, it's essential you give them clear feedback on where you see the gaps. Have a coaching conversation about what it would take to address those gaps and what level of progress you expect to see by when. Make it clear that it's their responsibility to find ways to close these gaps, but also clarify what support they can expect from you, such as increasing their exposure to board discussions, getting them a coach, or perhaps even sponsoring a part-time MBA.

Step 5: Benchmark their progress. It's critical to give them honest and timely feedback about how they're progressing and whether there remain any gaps that might cause you to hire someone above them. In my experience, if you have this conversation over a period of time, most people will come to accept the calibration. By doing this, if and when you decide to hire someone above them, the chances are much higher that they'll see it as an opportunity to learn and grow rather than just getting upset and quitting.

Too many CEOs avoid these discussions because they can't articulate what the future CXO needs to be able to do, because they value loyalty over performance, or most commonly because their AI filter tells them that these conversations will be too uncomfortable. As a result, the conversation happens way too late or not at all. But remember that the person you're "protecting" by skipping these conversations is yourself, not your leaders. You do them no favors by not giving them the best chance to keep up with the growth of your company.

And if they don't make it and you need to layer them under a CXO, can you still retain them as motivated and enthusiastic department heads? I've seen it many times—and you're a lot more likely to get there if you practice this ritual.

Recap

- In smaller organizations, department heads may have a range of titles, but the nature of their job remains similar—building and running a focused team.

- As organizations scale, they increasingly need true CXOs to contribute to the enterprise leadership. The role of a CXO requires spending less time on day-to-day departmental tasks and more on company-wide responsibilities.

- In particular, CXOs are key to building effective cross-functional collaboration at all levels, and should invest a significant amount of their time in designing and facilitating critical cross-functional work.

- CXOs also need to focus on how their departments will scale—this may not be as simple as hiring more people but may require reorganization or even reinvention.

- Not all departmental heads can grow into being true CXOs. This creates a dilemma for CEOs: Should they bring in someone above the departmental head and risk losing a long-serving trusted executive? Or should they allow them to continue as they are, and take the risk that they eventually fail?

- To prevent this dilemma, CEOs should hold regular conversations with their reports about where they are on the journey toward being a true CXO and identify any gaps they need to address.

- If these conversations are handled correctly, you'll get one of two happy outcomes: either the person grows enough to continue reporting directly to the CEO, or they'll welcome a CXO coming in above them, knowing that they can learn from that person.

Chapter 10

Rituals for Cross-Functional Collaboration

▼

In this chapter, we learn about the single most common pain point for high-growth companies: frictions between different departments that can grow into silos and prevent effective cross-functional collaboration.

RAILWAYZ PROVIDES SALESFORCE automation software for large corporates. After many years of struggling to get traction, in 2017 they really started to break through, and by 2020 their software was being used by twenty of the twenty-five largest salesforce employers in the United States.

Although designed to be a SaaS product, it turned out that customers demanded enormous amounts of customization and integration into other systems. This meant that many different RailWayz departments had to be involved. Starting with presales through the pilot and into full implementation and customer success, I counted nine different departments that had direct contact with their largest clients.

Clearly, their success depended on their ability to maintain seamless communications and collaboration across these departments. Unfortunately, this was far from the reality. Customers complained that their interactions with RailWayz were fragmented, inconsistent, and as a result, frustrating. But Joseph, the CEO, only recognized how serious a problem it was after a large customer terminated their contract and cited this as the main reason. This termination resulted in an explosion of blame-slinging arguments, at which point he contacted me to see what I could do to help.

My first move was to help them recognize that their customer touchpoints were so intertwined that they could never succeed at identifying who was "to blame" for what—or even where things went wrong. The root cause was far more complex than someone not doing their job well; it was a systemic and cultural issue rather than a single department's fault.

As we delved further into it, it became clear that egos, different working styles, misaligned goals, and a degree of favoritism from the founders all played a role in setting up the frequent clashes between departments. Realizing that the root causes were deeply ingrained, RailWayz's leadership team acknowledged the need for a drastic shift.

Together, we agreed that a new organizational design would help but that it wouldn't be enough unless we also changed the ways of working and the underlying culture of collaboration. Ten months and several workshops later, the transformation at RailWayz was largely complete. Collaboration was far better, and the most recent customer feedback had spiked upward.

Even if your business is a lot less complex than RailWayz and your team is a lot more collaborative, you're likely to encounter significant friction when it comes to cross-functional collaboration.

As your business scales, your capacity to take on more complex projects grows along with your growing expertise. But these projects can no longer be accomplished by a few people or a single department. This is the point at which frictionless cross-functional collaboration becomes a make-or-break capability.

Imagine you've been assigned to a new project that has half a dozen members from different departments. Everyone turns up at the first meeting showing enthusiasm and goodwill. You know some of the people well; others you're meeting for the first time, but they all seem great and easy to work with. You leave the kick-off meeting confident that the project will go just fine.

The potential for friction is rarely apparent on day one, but things rarely stay as rosy as this. Virtually all my clients have found cross-functional collaboration to be the single biggest source of organizational friction. It got so bad in one company that the CEO gave up on trying to resolve the interdepartmental conflicts and instead directed his executives to create parallel teams: the finance department hired its own engineers to develop the tools they needed, and the CRM team hired its own designers because they couldn't get what they needed from the marketing department. This, of course, led to duplication of effort, inconsistent approaches, and ultimately even more friction.

So, how does a cross-functional team go from the happy, shiny kick-off meeting to these kinds of problems? And why do these occur so much more frequently in cross-functional teams than in others?

Hidden Factors Make Cross-Functional Collaboration Hard

Within a single department, people typically share the same goals. They understand the priorities and tend to make the same trade-offs. When resources are tight, everyone knows and adjusts accordingly. They speak the same language and use lots of shorthand that everyone understands. And they have ample opportunities for informal chats, so it rarely takes more than a day to sort out any confusion or misunderstandings. None of these things is true in cross-functional teams. Instead:

- Different departments may have quite different goals and different priorities—but these may not be acknowledged or even apparent.

- One department may have plenty of resources to devote to a shared project, another barely any.

- There's generally more distance, both physical and psychological, between cross-functional counterparts, so communication doesn't happen unless someone consciously initiates it.

- Conversations are usually focused on "it" topics, so there are far fewer opportunities to build trusted relationships through "us" conversations.

- Since people don't have the same levels of trust, small misunderstandings and tensions often go unaddressed.

These challenges become more acute when people can't agree on a way forward. Within a department, two teammates who are having a disagreement can bring the issue to their (shared) boss, who clearly has the final authority. But in a cross-functional team, each person has a different boss, and it's often far from clear who would have the right to make the call. This can lead to a power struggle. More often, it leads to people avoiding the conflict altogether by kicking the issue down the road, causing progress to slow down.

This brings us to another challenge of cross-functional work: lack of accountability. Because each person reports to a different boss, it's all too easy for them to blame each other for any lack of success. And since neither boss has a complete picture of what's been happening, it's hard for them to hold their employees fully accountable.

On day one, all that goodwill and enthusiasm make it seem like the cross-functional team will do just fine. It's only over time that these hidden challenges and asymmetries make themselves felt as frictions.

Ritual 11:
Set Up Cross-Functional Work for Success

You can never overcome these structural challenges completely, but the cross-functional teams that have the most success are the ones who recognize the challenges up front and deal with them openly along the way. Remember that how you're viewing this new cross-functional project may be very different from how your colleagues view it. The purpose of this ritual is to build alignment based on a shared understanding of the context.

Step 1: Identify the key stakeholders. This may be the entire cross-functional team, or if the project involves many people, it can be the leaders of each subgroup.

Step 2: Ask each stakeholder to individually prepare their answers to these nine setup questions:

- What are the goals of this cross-functional project or process?

- Which of these goals is paramount? Is there an overarching mission for this project or process?

- How should we measure our progress? Are there both quantitative and qualitative measures? How will these be assessed or tracked?

- What are the key milestones or deadlines?

- Where does this project rank relative to each of your other responsibilities and commitments?

  ○ As high in priority as anything else I'm working on.

  ○ A relatively high priority but not the highest.

  ○ A relatively low priority.

- How much time do you anticipate you/your team spending on this project?

- What constraints on your ability to fulfill your role should others be aware of (for example, schedule time off, family commitments, or a major project due partway through)?

- How should the cross-functional team communicate?

  ○ How often should it meet?

  ○ Who should attend these meetings, and who should chair them?

  ○ What Slack channels or other communications media will help? How should they be used?

- If the team is unable to come to an agreement on an important issue, how and to whom should those be escalated or resolved?

Step 3: Get together and share your answers to each question. Discuss each point in turn, and let people share their thinking. Then ask if the point needs further discussion. Don't expect to have perfect alignment on day one. In many cases, it's enough to have a shared understanding, but some points may require a common resolution. If you can't come to an agreement on a point within ten minutes, keep going and flag it as an issue to keep an eye on or come back to. You can revisit these flagged issues down the road to see if they are causing tensions or problems.

Trust Problems Revisited

Real breakdowns in collaboration are typically interpersonal in nature—and these are more likely to happen in cross-functional contexts than in any other. Let's see how and why these breakdowns happen.

Meera was a product manager at Lido, an online concierge service. She worked closely with Aiden, who was a fellow product manager. They had developed a good relationship over the past two years, so when Aiden challenged her design work on a product during a team meeting, she didn't lose her cool. Instead, even though she disagreed, she assumed he had a valid reason to challenge it—as well as good intentions—so she resisted taking the bait. She calmed herself, asked a clarifying question, and responded constructively. After the meeting, she said to him that she found his comments a little aggressive, but they talked it through and were soon back on track.

But when Becks, a manager in the marketing department, challenged the same work in a cross-departmental meeting, Meera did lose her cool. She felt sure that Becks was doing this to avoid taking the blame for the poor initial results the product had had in the market—and she knew Becks was under pressure about it. So, she pushed back hard, told her she didn't understand what her problem was—and their relationship deteriorated from there.

What's the difference? In both cases, Meera was momentarily confused, paralyzed by what I call a WTF moment: "Why would they say that? What are they talking about?" When we don't have high trust in someone, we instinctively answer these WTF-type questions with negative assumptions and attributions.

"She doesn't get it," we might think. Or "He's too new here to know that that would never work." Or "She really isn't very smart." These are all attributions about the other person's *competence*.

Even worse, we frequently make assumptions about the other person's *motives*: "He's just covering his ass and trying to shift the blame to me," or "She'll do anything to shine in front of the boss."

Meera didn't make these assumptions about Aiden because she knew him well and trusted him, so in the instant that she calmed herself, she was able to give him the benefit of the doubt and act accordingly. But her reaction to Becks is, unfortunately, a very common one when someone we don't know well or fully trust says or does something that makes no sense to us.

Here's the even bigger problem: because Meera's attributions about Becks were negative ("She's just trying to cover for her own failed marketing campaign"), she could never share them openly because that would clearly be offensive and would damage their relationship. Put differently, her AI filter definitively ruled out having that conversation. Because she can't think of anything constructive to say, she won't say anything at all, and the episode will go undiscussed and unresolved.

She'll never know whether she was right or whether Becks had a legitimate concern. Instead, she'll continue to see Becks as a self-serving, political person who will say whatever she needs to in the moment—all based on one moment.

Ritual 12:
Managing Our WTF Moments

In short, our spontaneous reactions to WTF moments make us a prisoner in a jail cell of our own creation—in which a growing number of our colleagues are either incompetent or self-serving or both.

It turns out that this behavior is a universal bug: in the absence of trust, people tend to make negative assumptions about others' competence or motives when they say or do things we don't understand. It occurs in all cultures, organizations, and personality types. And it's certainly not specific to cross-functional contexts, but it's a bit more likely to arise in them because trust tends to be lower.

This entire process takes place in our mind instantaneously and unconsciously, so it's nearly impossible for us to see ourselves making these destructive leaps. Even worse, we generally share these negative, untested assumptions with others in the form of gossip (we're back at bucket 2, in the bar). We tell ourselves that's okay as long as we avoid the embarrassment and awkwardness of holding a direct conversation with the person who set off the chain of events. Left unchecked, this can lead to a toxic culture in which numerous staff "have a real problem" with others to the point where they can no longer work effectively.

The good news is there's a way out of this trap, and this ritual will show you how.

Step 1: Tune in to your confusion. We make these assumptions and attributions so quickly and unconsciously that we aren't even aware of having done it. So, the key is to tune in to the WTF moment itself—to experience that momentary feeling of confusion. Remember that it's just confusion, nothing more; someone has just said or done something that doesn't make sense to you. Then, to avoid jumping to conclusions, use what I call the 3 Cs framework: curious, confused, and concerned.

Step 2: "I'm curious . . . " Say this, followed by a question. The question almost doesn't matter—as long as it's a genuine one and not an attack:

- "Becks, I'm curious, what's your specific concern about the design?"

- "Vinod, I'm curious, what's the thinking behind your suggestion that we close our Taiwan office?"

- "Jennifer, I'm curious, just now you said we're going to need to reduce my head count for next year. But, as you know, the board said we need to prioritize this next year, so how do you reconcile these?"

Now breathe, relax, and listen. Don't worry too much about whether you agree or disagree. And don't interrupt. If their initial answer doesn't put your mind to rest, then go to . . .

Step 3: "I'm confused . . . " Again, say this followed by a question, such as:

- "I'm confused. I thought we had discussed and agreed on this. What led you to change your mind?"

- "I'm confused. Why do you think Taiwan isn't ever going to be profitable? Our forecast shows that it will be."

Whatever their answer, there's a good chance it won't fully

alleviate your worry. The key here is to avoid endless debate. Instead, keep asking questions, stay quiet, and listen. If a few questions don't lead you to a common understanding, now is the time to bring out "concerned."

Step 4: "I'm concerned . . . " Saying you're concerned is a powerful way to manage conflict. It acknowledges that the other person has a right to their point of view—that we accept they are not clueless or self-serving—but that we still disagree. It's also a good way of separating the elements of their argument that we *can* agree on from those we can't, which helps move the discussion forward. It might sound like this: "Vinod, I agree that Taiwan has been struggling and that in the short term the numbers look better off if we close it. But I'm concerned that this would damage our relationship with global customers who we promised to serve in Taiwan. How can we address this concern?"

We all have our WTF moments, but in the context of an important work relationship, they can be highly destructive. It's easy to walk away from WTF moments confident that our negative assumptions about the other person are *actually right* and that the problem lies with the other person: they're either incompetent or self-serving. But these moments are most often nothing more than a misunderstanding. We owe it to our colleagues and our company to try to unpick those moments and respond with curiosity instead of judgment.

Building Collaboration across Entire Teams

Until now, we've focused on cross-functional interactions involving a handful of individuals, but as your organization grows, these interactions can become large scale, involving two or more entire departments. These can take one of two forms:

- An internal supplier/customer relationship (e.g., the finance department supporting the sales department with lots of financial data and analysis).

- A true collaborative relationship (e.g., sales and customer success working together on customer onboarding).

If you're not careful, small tensions can grow into a structural tension where "everyone knows" departments A and B don't work well together. That's a situation you definitely want to avoid. To prevent this, use the following ritual.

Ritual 13:
Cross-Team Feedback

Sharing feedback at the team level can be a powerful and highly practical way of improving cross-functional collaboration. It helps to depersonalize any tensions or conflicts and instead focuses on some of the structural challenges: differences in priorities, workflows, ways of working, and so on.

Step 1: Identify the stakeholders. Identify the two or three departments that interact closely and whose success depends on the quality of their collaboration.

Step 2: Conduct surveys within each team. Ask the head of each department to conduct an anonymous survey with four or more team members who have significant experience in working with the other department. This should involve a short, written survey or a set of brief interviews. Either way, you want to keep it simple, so here are some questions I'd recommend.

- How would you evaluate the quality of the work department X does that your department depends or relies on? What specific suggestions do you have as to how they could improve?

- How would you evaluate department X's dependability? What specific suggestions do you have as to how they could improve?

- How would you evaluate department X's helpfulness? What specific suggestions do you have as to how they could improve?

- Overall, what score would you give department X in terms of how well they collaborate with your department?

- What other suggestions do you have about how department X and your department could collaborate more effectively? Be specific and constructive.

- What could your department do differently to improve collaboration?

Step 3: Department heads meet to synthesize and discuss. Synthesize the results, and have a discussion between the two department heads to decide which key messages to share with the broader teams. There's not much value in sharing a lot of raw data, especially if it's highly critical. People are much more likely to improve if they're asked to focus their efforts on one or two high-value shifts rather than sharing a lot of criticism or asking them to improve along multiple dimensions.

Step 4: Share feedback within teams. Each department head should share the high-level survey results and key takeaways with their own team. The teams should then discuss how they can take on board the feedback and improve. As with all feedback, it should be taken as suggestions—it's still up to each department to decide which items to act on and how.

Note: The process should be done mutually so that both departments share and receive feedback around the same time. If these types of interaction are crucial to your company's success, it would make sense to hold departmental heads responsible for improving their team's collaboration score.

As your company grows and organizational complexity accelerates, cross-functional collaboration becomes more and more likely to slow your company down. The obstacles to smooth collaboration may be invisible, but they're predictable if you know what to look for.

As your company grows and organizational complexity accelerates, cross-functional collaboration becomes more and more likely to slow your company down.

The rituals in this chapter will help you surface potential issues at the start of a collaboration, prevent misunderstandings from blowing up, and keep large-scale collaborations running smoothly. Don't wait for cross-functional collaboration to become a source of pain—start using these rituals as soon as this type of work becomes a frequent or ongoing feature of your organization. If you do, you'll save your organization from some of the most dangerous friction it faces on the path to full scale.

Recap

- Friction in cross-functional collaboration is the most common organizational challenge that high-growth companies face. It can be a major source of organizational underperformance, impacting customer satisfaction, project delivery, and other key outcomes—as well as the morale of your people.

- Hidden differences and asymmetries between teams, such as differing goals, resources, and information, as well as factors such as distance and lack of trust, make cross-functional collaboration harder than it looks.

- Because there is often lower trust in this context, misunderstandings can rapidly escalate. Learning to manage your WTF moments is a key skill for anyone working in high-stakes, high-stress situations.

- Many of these tensions can be anticipated and prevented using the Set Up Cross-Functional Work for Success Ritual (page 167).

- Interteam collaboration can also be improved by sharing feedback at the team level rather than at the individual level.

Chapter 11

Culture Building Rituals

▼

In this chapter, you'll learn how you can leverage core values to build a Productive and Positive culture. We'll also look at how easy it is for you and your top leadership to lose the trust of your staff as you grow and what you need to do to prevent that from happening.

NO DOUBT SOME READERS are wondering where company values fit into all this. In theory, they're the embodiment of a company's best wisdom on how its people should act—and interact with each other. But do they work?

Values statements have become increasingly standard fare both in traditional corporates and start-ups. They aim to articulate the principles that underpin the companies' ethos and culture. Commitments to integrity, innovation, customer service, and other worthy ideals are all very nice, but there's a growing realization that these exercises rarely have a meaningful impact. There are several reasons for this.

First, if you adopt values that aren't already largely true

within your organization, you're likely to generate a very cynical response—often within days—as your people witness behaviors and actions that are so obviously at odds with the stated values.

Second, values are often too vague or aspirational to be meaningful. If words like *integrity* or *innovation* aren't clearly defined and illustrated with relevant, specific examples of the behaviors you're looking for, your people will quicky forget about them.

More recently, some companies have adopted values in response to external pressures or social trends rather than in reflection of their actual beliefs. This lack of authenticity again leads to apathy, cynicism, or even a backlash.

Personally, I do believe that values statements have their place. They can have a positive influence on an organization's culture and behaviors but only when they're understood and used as one part of a broader, active approach to cultivating these behaviors. And that approach relies on continuous feedback (both positive and negative).

If you and your senior executives are not truly committed to commending positive examples of people living the company's values, *and* calling out people when stated values are not adhered to, then there's almost no chance they'll have an impact. But in companies (LinkedIn being a great example) where managers are both expected and trained to give this kind of continuous feedback, they can make a real difference.

The best way to think about company values is as a form of the Contracting for Feedback Ritual (page 130). If you embed your company values in the recruiting process, you can explain that a job with your company comes with a commitment to these values and a willingness to receive feedback when you fall short of them.

Naturally any eager recruit will agree to this, regardless of whether they're being genuine or just trying to land the job. But here's the thing: even if they weren't entirely honest, it still makes it much easier for you as their managers to one day say, "Hey, do you recall how we talked about [company value] and how I said we really took this seriously here? Great. Because I wanted to point out a couple of examples where I think you could have done better and highlight an example where I thought you really nailed it."

Not All Values Are Equal

Not all the ideals that companies often commit to are equally useful. Some are too vague, others are too disconnected from people's daily lives, and others are simply too different from the reality of how people currently behave to take hold. This observation led me to wonder if there are some essential values—values that absolutely must be in place if you're going to build a high-performance organization.

I believe there are.

Just as you can't have life without water, and you can't have water without the atomic elements of hydrogen and oxygen, I believe there are a few atomic values that are foundational to achieving the consistently high levels of Productivity and Positivity that underpin high performance. Here they are:

> There are a few atomic values that are foundational to achieving the consistently high levels of Productivity and Positivity.

1. Intellectual humility. Intellectual humility is the deep conviction that neither you nor anyone else has, or can have, a monopoly on the truth. No one can ever be 100 percent right because no single person can see the complete picture. No matter how confident you are in your perspective, you remain humble enough to recognize that you might be partly wrong or be missing a piece of the puzzle. This doesn't mean you don't form strong views or advocate passionately for them. It means you articulate your views as hypotheses, invite others to test or challenge them, and remain open to hearing disconfirming evidence. This approach is best summarized by the phrase "strong opinions, loosely held."

2. **Empathy.** At one level, empathy is a practical skill that can easily be learned—in fact, the quality of listening embedded in many of the rituals in this book is the very embodiment of empathy. But ultimately, empathy stems from a deeper belief: that the emotional experiences of other people matter—and that these experiences aren't necessarily going to line up with your expectations or what you experience in the same situation. Empathy is a key atom in any high-trust relationship, and as we've seen, these relationships are key to the success of your organization.

3. **Psychological safety.** Psychological safety has become a bit of a buzzword: people agree that it's important without being entirely clear on what it is or how to create it. But if people don't feel comfortable challenging others' views, giving feedback, or just being themselves, then it's going to be tough to generate the quality of both the "it" and "us" conversations you're going to need.

4. **Courage.** Courage is the flip side of psychological safety: it's about frank, direct, bold, and sincere communication. It doesn't mean everyone has to say everything on their

minds, but, as we learned in chapter 6, it's a necessary ingredient in the "us" conversations that enable us to diagnose and fix frictions.

Atoms into Molecules

Companies naturally adopt a wide variety of values, and these don't necessarily have to include the atomic four explicitly—though I'd suggest they do. These atomic values are the building blocks of a high-performance culture: and when they're weak, some of the most common values that companies commit to also tend to be weak. That's because the "molecular level" values they're hoping to create *depend* on these atomic values. If one essential atom is weak or missing, the chemistry just doesn't work.

For example, teamwork requires a combination of empathy and intellectual humility. Empathy enables people to connect with and relate to each other, and intellectual humility allows them to listen deeply and build on each other's ideas.

Innovation absolutely requires courage and psychological safety. Without these, no one will share the radical or "stupid" ideas you need to create your future.

Diversity and inclusiveness—values we hear a lot about these days—require psychological safety, empathy, and intellectual humility. We have to get past the numbers side of diversity (i.e., the percentage of women or BIPOC employees). Having a diverse group in the room doesn't do anyone any good unless everyone feels able to contribute and have an influence. There are *many* reasons why they might not feel this—not just race and gender but also cultural background, personality type, language skills, seniority, and others. Psychological safety is crucial for getting everyone to speak up, and intellectual humility and empathy help ensure that even "diverse" contributions are taken seriously.

Now we can see why so many companies struggle to live up to their values—they're missing some essential atoms.

For example, I've worked with software companies populated by large numbers of highly technical people who were often quite introverted. Intellectual humility was common in these companies, but empathy was in short supply. The result was that only close coworkers tended to form high-trust relationships. So, as they scaled beyond a few small teams, a fair amount of friction crept into their organizations. Referring back to the Productivity and Positivity matrix, these tend to be Intimidating companies (high on Productivity, low on Positivity).

I've also seen companies with Comforting cultures (high on Positivity, low on Productivity). The root cause? Lack of courage.

So, ask yourself this: Which of the atomic values is weak in your company? Don't expect to be able to truly live your values if these non-negotiable values are weak. Instead, acknowledge the weak spots and bring them into focus. By adopting the right rituals, you can strengthen these, and you'll soon see your other values start to come to life, too.

Maintaining Your Culture in Tough Times

The COVID-19 pandemic severely hit Airbnb. With global travel coming to a near halt, the company saw its bookings and revenues plummet. In May 2020, CEO Brian Chesky made the painful decision to lay off nearly 25 percent of Airbnb's workforce, about 1,900 employees.

"I think the psychology of the leader often becomes the psychology of the organisation," said Chesky in May 2021, reflecting on a year in which his company was thrown into disarray by the global pandemic.

What set Chesky apart was his approach to this crisis. He

communicated openly with his employees, detailing the reasons for the layoffs in a letter that he also made public. He offered generous severance packages, extended healthcare benefits, and allowed laid-off US employees to keep their company laptops, key in a market where most job interviews were remote. He also launched an alumni talent directory to help laid-off employees find new jobs.

Not every company could afford to do that—but much of what he did cost nothing. He sent out personal emails and video messages to Airbnb's hosts, guests, and employees, acknowledging the challenges and reassuring them of Airbnb's commitment to their well-being. In these messages, he emphasized that their core values would be the basis on which they made difficult decisions.

While it was a painful period, Chesky's empathetic, transparent, and supportive approach during the crisis significantly helped maintain trust among employees and the public. As travel started to rebound, Airbnb was well positioned to recover, culminating in a successful IPO in December 2020. As of this writing, Airbnb has an overall Glassdoor rating of 4.2 out of 5, and 97 percent of their employees would recommend working at Airbnb to a friend.

If you're growing fast, it means you're doing a lot right and putting wins on the board regularly. Conveying all the good news about what's happening is natural, and senior leaders naturally lean into these communications. But even the most successful companies hit obstacles—large or small—that result in not-so-good news: executives who have to be let go, budgets that need to be tightened, closed product lines, or delayed expansion plans.

The way these moments are communicated will largely determine how much trust your staff have in the company leadership.

In a Day Zero organization, staff have plenty of opportunities to interact with the senior leaders. They hear your thoughts directly and have the chance to ask you questions. So, if they picked up on some news that confuses or concerns them, there's a good chance they'll address it quickly and hear the truth from the horse's mouth.

But as your company grows, your people get more and more of their information from gossip—and their managers may not be in a position to credibly clarify the reality. That makes it much easier for them to lose confidence or trust in the company when things aren't going well.

In a scaling organization, it's important to think strategically about how to maintain trust and open communication between senior leaders and all staff. Town halls, group Slacks, all-staff emails, blogs, and videos can all be effective communication media; and most companies are skillful at using them to celebrate successes, announce milestones, introduce new team members, and keep people abreast of what's happening. Sharing good news is easy—but it's how you handle tough or bad news that determines how much trust your people will have in your leadership.

Most founders aren't sure how to go about sharing potentially bad or upsetting news—like the fact that an executive had to be let go, a fundraising round that's been postponed, or a possible setback with a regulator. Too often, they simply avoid any communication or mishandle these situations in a way that undermines trust in the company or its leadership. Let's look at why this works less well than you'd imagine and how to handle these situations in a way that builds trust between your staff and the company leadership instead of undermining it.

Nature Abhors a Vacuum

It's easy to understand why you might be reluctant to address negative issues publicly. In a Zoom call with hundreds of participants, it's hard to know how people will react to anything other than good news. You're concerned that sharing uncertainties or bad news might worry or distract people, and what good would that do? It looks like there's more downside than upside.

In some cases, that's true. But in others, it turns out to be completely wrong. Let's look at two examples.

Carl, the CEO of Pandoo, a five-hundred-person company in the health-tech sector, hired three new executives—and then exited two of them within months of their joining. He just felt they weren't the right fit, and he believed in firing fast. He recognized this didn't reflect very well on his hiring abilities but decided that letting them go was better than letting mis-hires hang around.

Carl never said anything publicly about what was happening. One day, the new executive would just be gone, and only their direct reports would be notified. The rest of the staff never heard anything from the company about what was going on—all they could see was the revolving door at the top. Carl thought that talking about it would distract people as well as reflect poorly on him, and that by keeping it quiet, he was minimizing drama and sending the message that people should stay focused on their work.

Unsurprisingly, that's not how it played out. In the absence of clear and credible explanations for what had happened, his staff invented all kinds of stories: Was the company going broke? Had it canceled its expansion plans? Or was the CEO just completely mercurial, blowing hot one day and cold the next? If so, were they also at risk of being fired on a whim? The more lurid the stories, the more time people spent gossiping about them.

Ironically, a similar thing happened at a company where the CEO *failed* to remove people who everyone knew needed to go. The company was known for its ultra Positive (but not very Productive) culture, including plenty of foosball tables and breakfast cereal. Everyone was aware that investors were pressuring the founders to cut the burn rate—it had even made it into the press. Much earlier, the company had gone on a not-very-disciplined hiring spree and brought in a bunch of recent university grads. The more experienced people saw clearly that many of the new grads weren't doing much apart from enjoying the foosball and cereal, so everyone was connecting the dots and expecting a layoff that would help the company get back on track financially.

But nothing happened. The leadership team needed to make cuts—had even discussed making cuts behind closed doors—but months later, they still hadn't been executed. There were some valid reasons for this that had to do with the company's reputation with the local government (which had invested in the company), but no one knew about this sensitivity. Throughout this period, no senior executive spoke with the staff about the media articles, the burn rate, or the (non) layoffs. People wondered what was going on and questioned whether the leadership had the courage to right the ship or whether they'd all go down together.

As you can see, the issue here isn't about what the leadership *does*. In one case management was "brutal" and fired people at the drop of a hat. In the other, management was "too soft" and failed to fire people even when they needed to. What matters is how effectively the decision is explained.

Why did these CEOs miscalculate so badly? Because they failed to recognize that nature abhors a vacuum. When people are aware that something is brewing, saying nothing only makes things worse. People naturally fill the silence with their worst assumptions and wildest conspiracy theories— we're back at bucket 2 conversations at the bar. They'll generally imagine that things are much worse than the truth, which spreads angst and worry throughout the organization.

Actually, it's worse. When senior leaders don't communicate transparently about something everyone is aware of, staff also start to wonder what else their leaders might be hiding. They think, "If they won't address this thing that's obvious to everyone, what other problems are they sweeping under the rug? Is the company in trouble? Should we be polishing our CVs?"

Ritual 14:
Maintain Connection and Transparency

Trust in leadership deteriorates amazingly fast when staff perceive a lack of transparency. So even if the situation is evolving and the facts aren't all in yet, it's better to acknowledge what's happening. Maintaining open communication with your staff is crucial to maintaining their trust when times are tough—even if you can't share all of what's happening. This ritual will help you work through uncertain times or bad news while building rather than eroding trust.

Step 1: Anticipate, listen, and proactively plan for issues before they become a crisis. If you think people might be worried about an issue or talking about it at the bar, they almost certainly are. It's crucial for you to know what the sentiment on the ground is, so make sure people have confidential ways to share their concerns and feedback. That could either be via an anonymous online platform or through trusted managers or HR personnel. Have you created enough trust with your managers so that they will be open with you as well, even when what they have to share might reflect poorly on you?

Adopt a traffic light system as a threshold for reaction (e.g., red means you need to take action now, amber means wait and see, and green means proceed but drive with care). As a rule of thumb, it's generally safer to get out in front of any brewing issues or gossip with a clear perspective and message than to wait too long.

Step 2: Acknowledge the issue. "Many of you might have noticed or heard that . . . " If there's uncertainty around the issue—for example, you don't yet know whether your expected funding will come through—say so. Let them know when you will have more clarity, and commit to sharing updates in a timely manner. If there's information you can't share (for example, an executive left and it wouldn't be appropriate to reveal why), say so. People will accept that they can't know everything if you're straight about what they can know. Be careful not to overmessage or make lots of promises.

In some situations, it's also a good idea to invite suggestions on how to handle the situation from your staff. Remember that your people on the frontline understand better than you how an issue is likely to be seen by your customers. Your teams will respect you more if you ask for and listen to their feedback and suggestions.

Step 3: Explain what you're doing about it. Describe how the leadership team is engaging with the issue and how you plan to respond to it or resolve it. Show that you're taking it seriously and giving it the consideration it deserves. Be clear on timelines and when they can expect the next update.

Step 4: Express confidence in the future. Reassure people—in an honest way—that everything will work out. There may be some tough times ahead or hard decisions to make, but the company will survive this setback or resolve this uncertainty and come out stronger.

This isn't an argument for maximum transparency about everything at all times. If the issue isn't worrying people or a topic for the bar, there's no reason to make it one. But remember that trust is an essential element of a Productive and Positive culture. The same principles you learned in chapter 6 still apply—it just takes different approaches to build and maintain trust in this context.

It may seem like this interaction is less important than those we dealt with in previous chapters—but imagine yourself in your staff's position. How does it feel to go to work every day wondering if your leaders are being straight with you? The doubt or mistrust that creeps in is subtle, but it can have a huge impact on people's commitment.

On the flip side, when leaders build trust by openly addressing important issues, it creates a powerful sense of connection that helps people across a large organization stay aligned and committed. This can make the difference between an organization that stalls in a difficult period and never fully recovers and one that goes on to regain its high performance, as Airbnb did.

Recap

- Trust between a company's top leadership and staff tends to emerge naturally in a small organization. But as you grow, it's important that you carefully cultivate and protect this trust because, once damaged or lost, it's very difficult to rebuild.

- Transparency in communication is crucial to maintain trust between staff and top leadership especially in challenging or uncertain times.

- Failure to address negative events or rumors tends to make things worse. Staff often end up assuming the worst and indulge in destructive gossip.

- It's better to acknowledge and communicate about ongoing issues, even if all the facts are not yet available or you can't share them all, rather than staying silent and allowing assumptions to spread.

- Building and maintaining trust through open communication helps create a sense of unity within the organization. That can help you navigate any tough times.

Chapter 12

The
Ever-Growing CEO

▾

In this chapter, you'll learn about the essential shifts that every CEO must make to lead a truly scalable, high-performance organization—and how you can start building those skills and mindset, starting today.

WHEN I FIRST MET JOE CASK, the founder and CEO of SuperTrade, a B2B e-commerce business, his company had about one hundred people. Like most founders, Joe was ultrafocused on growth and spent most of his time on strategy, fundraising, and wooing iconic customers. He was in his element in all of these and was doing a great job—and was happy to work sixty-plus hours a week. SuperTrade was growing revenues at 100 percent a year. So, when I pitched him on my services, figuring he had no issues, he politely declined.

SuperTrade's head count was also doubling, so it wasn't long until the company was three hundred employees across eight countries. Joe felt that this rate of hiring helped him stay ahead of the competition—he liked to say "more people, more progress." But by now he found himself working seventy hours or more a week, racing from one meeting to another. His CHRO had been advising him for ages to step back from the day-to-day, but every time he tried that, things just fell apart, and he would jump back in, privately feeling satisfied that he was the glue that kept the company together.

Things continued like this until the day his wife threatened to leave him if he didn't spend more time at home. That worked. Having finally acknowledged that his leadership model wasn't scaling, he dedicated himself to getting his organization to perform at its full potential and rely less on him. But lacking a clear approach, he ended up playing Whack-a-Mole—solving one organizational problem only for another two or three others to crop up in its place. When he finally hired me, he admitted with a sheepish look that his new thinking was "more people, more problems."

Compare Joe with Hailey Kristiansen, who recently took her property portal company public for just under a billion dollars. That's a wonderful achievement by itself, but what's truly amazing is that for the two years leading up to this milestone, she's been working a four-day week. Her company, Pacific Grove, has the best margins in her industry, outstanding ratings on Glassdoor, and an enviably low employee turnover rate.

How did she do it? And what was different about her approach compared to Joe's?

Hailey set out to build an organization that could run itself even when she wasn't there—not because she didn't like her job as CEO but because she recognized that whatever the organization needed to tackle this year, it would have to do the same plus much more in the coming years. Instead of spending her time holding business reviews, pursuing new commercial opportunities, and fixing operational hiccups, she focused on building the right team of executives: people who could run those reviews, land those opportunities, and deal with the hiccups better than she could.

When her company had been much smaller, she'd been right there in the thick of it. But over time, she built an organization and a culture that no longer needed her to do that. She now sees her job as setting the vision and strategy, dealing with investors and external stakeholders, and shaping the organization and culture—plus handing all the unexpected things that come with growth.

All this didn't happen in a day or a year. She's been pursuing this path for seven years and feels there is still some way to go. Her personal guideline is that she should give up at least 25 percent of what she does every year to create capacity for the next phase of growth.

It's not news that leaders of high-growth businesses need to evolve their roles. Fred Wilson, the renowned VC, says that every start-up will need to either reinvent or replace its core team three times on its way to scale.[7] Molly Graham, formerly of Google and Facebook, says that to build a rapidly scaling business, leaders need to give away their job every few months.[8]

Hailey, Fred, and Molly are all talking about the same thing: the need for leaders to evolve—even reinvent themselves—to stay ahead of the exploding complexity that growth brings.

Unfortunately, most leaders get stuck at a certain level and find they're unable to evolve further. Many feel the need to

---

[7] Fred Wilson. "MBA Mondays: Turning Your Team." AVC, August 12, 2013, avc.com/2013/08/mba-mondays-turning-your-team.

[8] "'Give Away Your Legos' and Other Commandments for Scaling Start-ups." *First Round Review*, Accessed July 8, 2022, review.firstround.com/give-away-your-legos-and-other-commandments-for-scaling-startups.

be in the weeds, make all the key decisions, or stay loyal to a particular team. To maximize your organization's scalability, as well as your own growth as a CEO, you'll need to understand the three mindsets that CEOs can have about their job.

The Action Mindset: Getting Stuff Done

In a Day Zero organization, leaders are all about getting stuff done—and that's as it should be. There are prototypes to design, customers to win, and investors to woo. It's all hands on deck, and everyone does a bit of everything, so even though your title may be CEO or CXO, you're as much an individual contributor as you are a manager. Your mindset is all about *action*.

If you were to make a pie chart showing the brain of an action mindset CEO—that is, where they focus their attention—it would look something like figure 12.1.

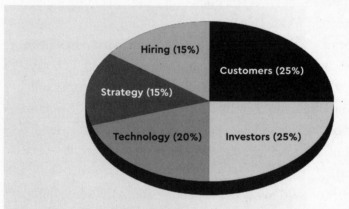

Figure 12.1. The action mindset.

But what happens when you keep this mindset as your company grows? Like Joe Cask, many CEOs love to keep their hands dirty long after their company has grown beyond Day Zero. They take pride in leading from the front. They talk to customers, work on the product road map, and run their own financial analysis. They're happy to work all hours of the day and night, often believing they can do most jobs better than their subordinates. And in some cases, they may even be right. But the obvious problem with the action mindset is this: it doesn't scale.

The Control Mindset: Making Sure Stuff Gets Done

Once an organization is mature enough that it has experts and managers across all the key functions, there are a lot fewer things that senior leaders have to do themselves. Marketing programs can be designed, salesforces hired, technology built, and financials analyzed by the people who are paid to do that.

But if you have the *control* mindset, you still worry: Will they do it well? On time? In the way that you want it to be done? Will they see all the angles? Unlike action-focused leaders, control-focused leaders don't spend as much time getting stuff done—instead, they spend almost all their energy *making sure it gets done.* Figure 12.2 illustrates what the brain of a control mindset CEO looks like.

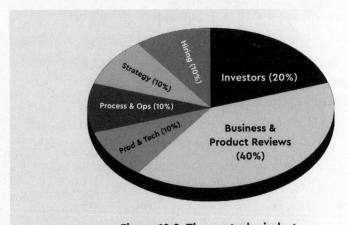

Figure 12.2. The control mindset.

Control leaders spend the bulk of their time checking, chasing, and challenging work done by others. This means lots of business, product, and project review meetings. They also spend time designing systems that help them feel confident that things are getting done—systems such as OKRs, budgets, and project trackers. Their role is akin to an über project manager, overseeing all aspects of the work being done in their organizations.

The good news is that a control mindset allows for much more scalability than the action mindset. The bad news is that it doesn't allow for nearly enough.

The Scaling Mindset: Building the Organization That Gets Stuff Done

If you're the CEO of a company growing from one hundred to several hundred or several thousand employees, you'll certainly experience explosive growth in your organization's complexity and the numerous problems this complexity creates. Early on, you knew exactly where things stood, what the obstacles to progress were, and who could fix them. Now you don't. Every holdup entails multiple people and teams with different perspectives and priorities.

When something needs to get done or fixed, it's no longer as simple as asking someone to do it—it now takes five or ten people working together to get it done; and this requires role clarity, coordination, good communications, trust—factors you didn't need to think about in the past.

This catches leaders off-guard, because the problems are below the surface. They're no longer about identifying who is "screwing up"—rather, they stem from how people, teams, and departments are interacting. Before, the solution to a technical holdup was hiring another developer with a particular set of skills. Now, the solution is helping the engineering team figure out how to support three different product lines. It's all harder to grasp and subtler to resolve.

Imagine what it's like to be the CEO of a huge company like Apple or Amazon. How can you add value to the thousands of tasks being done at any time? How can you oversee them? The answer, of course, is that you can't. So how do you add value to such a large enterprise?

By *building the organization* that gets the job done.

That's why the scaling mindset is fundamentally different. Your role is not to get stuff done, or even to make sure stuff gets done, but to create an organization and culture that reliably and sustainably produces the results you need. Since problems are way too multifaceted for you to fix, you need an organization that can diagnose and resolve its own problems.

> **Your role is not to get stuff done, or even to make sure stuff gets done, but to create an organization and culture that reliably and sustainably produces the results you need.**

This means that organizational development and culture are now your *most important* priorities, which is a massive shift from the action and control mindsets. You're now doing almost no hands-on problem-solving or oversight work. Instead, you spend your time communicating the vision, coaching your executives, addressing organizational conflicts, and facilitating effective cross-functional collaboration. You've gone from thinking about maximizing output to maximizing organizational effectiveness, which is a completely different mindset with a completely different attention pie chart.

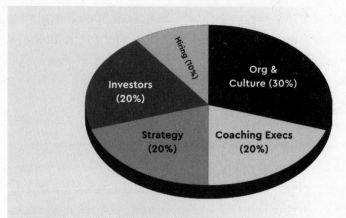

Figure 12.3. The scaling mindset.

Most leaders make the transition from the action to control mindset naturally and intuitively. But the transition to the scaling mindset is much harder.

The Two-Eyed CEO

Leaders with an action or control mindset focus relentlessly on tasks—but not on the organization executing those tasks. Typically, the only organizational factors they really pay attention to are the acute problems, like urgent hiring needs or executives who are threatening to leave. I call them one-eyed CEOs because they see every issue as a *business* issue.

But many "business" issues are organizational issues in disguise. When customer churn at RailWayz increased, it sure looked like a critical business issue—but at its root was the inability of the different teams to work seamlessly together. When too many of your key projects show delays, your engineering team didn't build quite what you needed, or your HR director says you're losing talent to the competition, these all seem like business problems . . . and, of course, they are. But they're also symptoms.

Sadly, many executives secretly thrive on this state of affairs because the constant flow of business problems reaching their desks makes them feel smart and useful and involved. But leaders with a scaling mindset understand that their job is not to solve these problems but rather to build an organization that either prevents them from happening or solves them lower in the organization. They recognize that by jumping in to solve problems, they are allowing some weakness or dysfunction in their organization to persist. When they do that, they undermine the scalability of their business.

As tempting as it is to dive in and fix things, scaling CEOs are incredibly rigorous in deciding which problems are truly theirs to solve. If it's a business problem that is rightly theirs, fine. But if it's a problem that should have been resolved at a lower level, or one that is a symptom of an organizational dysfunction, then a scaling executive will resist the temptation to jump in and solve it and focus instead (or, at minimum, in parallel) on addressing its organizational root cause.

In short, scaling CEOs always operate with two eyes open: one that is looking at issues through a traditional business problem-solving lens, the other through an organizational development lens. Their great skill is to assess which perspective brings the problem into clearer focus and is more likely to lead to long-term scalability. Then they act accordingly.

Scaling CEOs Need OQ

Nikola Tesla, one of the most prolific inventors in history, was known for his extraordinary intellectual abilities, including a powerful visualization technique. He was able to design, assemble, and test sophisticated inventions in his mind before even sketching a single diagram.

Tesla was the inventor of the alternating current motor. According to reports, Tesla designed the entire motor in his mind and then "ran" it mentally to observe its operation. After a certain period, he would check the machine in his mind to see which parts were wearing out. This ability to test and refine his inventions in his mind's laboratory before creating a physical prototype was a remarkably efficient way of developing new technologies.

Predicting how a new invention will perform by running it in your mind's eye is surely beyond most of our abilities. But as the leader of a scaling organization, it's vital that you're able to anticipate how your organization will perform as it adjusts to change, and what might cause it to develop frictions. I call this skill organizational intelligence, or OQ.

You already know about emotional intelligence. EQ is a measure of your ability to read, predict, and influence how people feel about different things. If you're interacting with a small group of people, EQ is all you need. But when you're a leader in a company with hundreds or thousands of staff spread across multiple locations, you need OQ.

Think of it as the ability to cast your EQ across larger groups of people and over time.

Let's say you're in a meeting you don't normally attend. Ted, a senior manager, speaks aggressively toward Sadiq, a junior manager from a different department, accusing him of having done sloppy work on the issue but not providing any illustration. The meeting accomplishes what it needed to despite Ted's behavior, and Ted's behavior was not that bad, so it would be easy enough to overlook it. If you have good EQ, you might want to check in with Sadiq after the meeting to see how he's feeling or ask someone else to do so. A bit more EQ might have you wondering whether Ted's behavior also left other attendees feeling uncomfortable and unsure how to handle it.

But if you have high OQ, you'll also think about that meeting in the broader context of the company's culture. If Ted is behaving that way and no one seems surprised by it, how many other people might he have left feeling bruised? And how many other managers might be behaving in the same way?

And if you haven't heard about this kind of thing, what does that say about the company culture? Could this kind of behavior cause the company to lose valuable employees? Has it already? How would you know?

This way of thinking—OQ in action—leads to a very different set of questions and future actions on your part—perhaps in this case asking HR to train people in how to maintain psychological safety.

Or imagine that one of your top executives proposes a new process for managing your largest accounts. You ask a number of questions about how it will affect customers, but she's clearly thought it through and has a number of customer anecdotes that support her proposal. But as someone with high OQ, you've already set this process running in your mind's eye, and it's led you to ask more questions: about how it's likely to affect other parts of the organization and whether they've been consulted on the proposal.

Ritual 15:
Become a Two-Eyed Leader

Leaders with excellent OQ can see how apparently straightforward things—like a change to a company policy, the launch of a new product, or the hiring of a new executive—might affect people and teams across their organization. Maintaining Productivity and Positivity as your business scales involves applying your OQ to dozens of situations like these—so let's see how you can get better at it with this ritual.

Every time one of your people brings you a business

problem that they're asking you to solve or give an opinion on, ask yourself this: What would it have taken for the organization to have anticipated and prevented this problem or to have resolved it without my help?

Take a minute to think about how that might have happened in an ideal world, and then ask yourself how realistic it is to expect your organization to be able to do that given its current level of maturity. This will lead you to one of three responses:

- Treat the issue as a business issue. If there's no clear way that your organization could have prevented this issue from reaching your desk, then it's probably yours to deal with rather than a sign of some organizational weakness.

- Address the issue as a business issue now, but think about how the organization can be strengthened in the medium term to prevent business issues like this one from reaching your desk in the future.

- Focus your response not on the business issue that has been pushed to you but on understanding the underlying organizational weakness that led to it. What could have prevented it? How could it have been spotted earlier? Who could have resolved it other than you?

To help your team understand your questions, explain that unless the organization is unable to prevent or resolve issues like this at a lower level, the company will be unable to scale—and engage them in identifying and addressing the organizational root causes.

Solutions could involve coaching someone to act more autonomously, clarifying responsibilities, or improving communications between different stakeholders involved in the issue.

Here are some questions you can ask yourself that will help you decide whether to approach this as a business or an organizational issue:

- **Have I seen this problem before?** If a business problem keeps recurring, it's likely that there's an underlying organizational issue behind it.

- **Is everyone working toward the same goals?** Sometimes business problems crop up because people are not pulling in the same direction. It's nearly impossible to collaborate effectively when people have different priorities or goals.

- **Are the right people making the decisions? And can they do this effectively?** A disagreement over what to do might really be a fight over who gets to choose. In some cases, the solution is as simple as clarifying who owns this particular decision. In others, it will need to be a joint decision—in which case the people involved need to find better ways of communicating. Bring the right people together and facilitate a dialogue that is both Productive and Positive until you are confident they can do it without you. With the right guidance, they can solve this problem—and many more in the future—without you.

- **Does the left hand know what the right hand is doing?** As your organization grows, it becomes harder for people to know what's going on. As a result, people take actions without consulting or informing others who should have been involved. This frequently causes business problems to land on your desk. That's a red flag that your company's communication skills aren't keeping up with its growth.

If you're looking to improve your OQ, in addition to practicing the Become a Two-Eyed Leader Ritual, it can also be helpful to identify someone in your organization who *does* have high OQ and bring them into your inner circle. Make them your radar, eyes, and ears for organizational health problems, and you'll soon learn to see things through "two eyes," as they do.

Ritual 16:
Give Away Your Legos

Molly Graham was a member of hypergrowth teams in the early days of Google and Facebook. She describes the incredible fun that leaders have in these situations because they're given so many Legos (people, resources, responsibilities) and can build almost anything they want. But as these leaders' teams scale, team members need to take over the Lego blocks that you had been playing with—otherwise the organization doesn't scale. The problem she saw was that leaders frequently resisted giving away their Legos—because they're fun to play with, familiar, and give them a sense that they're adding value. This ritual will help you learn to give your Legos away. If you're a CEO or a senior leader, I recommend you run this ritual every six months or so.

Start by choosing a representative month in your diary, and go through all your activities. Then take note of the following:

- Bucket your time according to the major categories of activities—whatever makes most sense to you. Buckets could be along the lines of strategy, operations, marketing, investors, business reviews, and coaching. The goal here is for you to understand where your time goes.

- Assign an average value to the time spent, where 5 is potentially game changing, and 1 is low.

- For each block of time, ask yourself this: Could this have been delegated?

- If the answer is yes, consider running an experiment in which you try to delegate this activity for a period of time.

- If the answer is no, ask yourself why. If the main reason is that you don't trust anyone lower in the organization to take on the task or make the decision, ask yourself if you are comfortable continuing to perform this activity for-ever—even as your company continues to scale. If not, you know you have a weakness that needs to be addressed.

- Develop an action plan that would free you from at least 10 percent of the commitments that absorbed your time in that six-month period.

In a Day Zero organization, you're naturally going to have an action mindset. As a result, the ratio of business to organizational problems you face is probably twenty to one.

With a control mindset, you're still focused on business issues, but you're more aware of organizational challenges and more involved in addressing them. By this point you should have already given away quite a few of your Legos as well. So, you might find that your ratio is five to one.

But if you're a scaling CEO who has given away a lot of their Legos, you'll probably find that the right ratio in terms of viewing issues through the business versus the organizational lens is around two to one or even one to one.

The more organizational problems you solve, the more

business problems can get resolved without you. Learning to be a great organization builder (and doctor) is how you become a true scaling CEO. Even better, it's how you get out of the way of your company's future growth.

Recap

- Most CEOs find it easy to transition from an action mindset to a control mindset, and this can take them and their organizations quite a distance.

- However, to truly build a large-scale company, CEOs need to make the much harder transition to the scaling mindset.

- This requires that they give up a large part of one of the roles they have probably found most satisfying: solving business problems. As long as they solve those problems, they're perpetuating the dependence of an organization that doesn't solve them.

- The scaling mindset involves focusing instead on creating the organization that can effectively anticipate and address complex business problems as the company grows.

- CEOs with a scaling mindset operate with two lenses: a business problem-solving lens and an organizational development lens.

- Scaling CEOs (and CXOs) should strengthen their organizational intelligence (OQ) in order to better anticipate how organizational frictions may develop and to ensure the smooth functioning of the company.

Chapter 13

Rituals to Create the Right Interactions

▼

In this chapter, you'll learn how you can orchestrate the key inter-actions that will keep your company moving forward using meeting design in concert with organizational design. You'll also learn how to keep everyone feeling strongly connected to the mothership as the company grows.

THROUGHOUT THIS BOOK, we've seen how the quality of interactions across your organization drive both Pro-ductivity and Positivity. They're what enable you to get the best out of your people, build high-performing teams, run cross-functional processes, and develop the next wave of talent that will allow your business to scale.

In a Day Zero company, great interactions take place organically. But as your company becomes much larger, it's *your* job as a leader to ensure that the right interactions are taking place with the right frequency and that there are as few barriers as possible to this happening. This is where organization design come in. But before we learn how and when to redesign your organizational structure, let's clarify what organizational design is really all about.

The Purpose of Organizational Design

People often think organizational design is primarily about decision rights. Decision rights are certainly important, but they aren't the only issue. Let's look at how things work at Picardin, a deep tech company making nanocoatings for the electronics industry.

Like most companies, when Picardin was small, it had a simple, functional organization. However, over the years it grew well beyond its base in Asia to include sales offices in the United States and Europe. It developed multiple products. And it sold to different types of customers, including OEM contract manufacturers as well as branded device manufacturers.

Sam was the product VP responsible for AquaShield, the company's proprietary waterproofing coating system. He had recently developed a new strategy to accelerate sales in the coming years. His main idea was to shift to a "razor and blades" strategy where they would start selling the coating equipment at a much-reduced price (close to break-even) but increase the price of their proprietary coating material. The profit impact of this would be negative in the short term, but Sam felt confident that the increased market penetration would pay off in the long term.

Now he was starting to think how he could get everyone aligned and felt daunted by the task. He had to get the regional managing directors (MDs) from Europe, the United States, and Asia to buy in. He also needed the buy-in of the channel directors (who ran the OEM and device channels respectively) and the CFO. Sam had been told by his CEO that he owned the strategy, so he figured the ultimate decision was his. But he knew he wouldn't get anywhere if he didn't have the full backing of all the key stakeholders.

In fact, all these people had a huge stake in the decision. The CFO was going to have to bear the short-term profit impact. The regional MDs were responsible for the sales organizations, and their necks would be on the line if the longer-term payoff didn't come through. And the channel directors had the deepest understanding of the industry forces facing their end customers and how their products impacted their customers' strategic position.

The decision rights approach to organizational design asks: Who is best placed to make this decision? But this example shows the limits of this approach. While it certainly speeds up decision-making to know that one person can make the final call, Sam's situation is very much the norm: building alignment among stakeholders is almost always essential, regardless of who has the final say. If Sam uses his decision rights to jam it down the others' throats, that's only going to be speedy in the narrowest sense of the word—it won't lead to effective execution. Instead, it will be the *quality* of their discussions that determines both the quality of the final strategy and the level of buy-in of the key stakeholders.

Now let's look at organizational design from a different perspective, that of optimizing interactions among people.

Let's return to Picardin and visit Maya, head of marketing for AquaShield in Europe, and ask a different question: Who does Maya need to interact with most intensively, day in and day out, to be effective at her job? Should she report to Sam, since he has the deepest understanding of the product strategy? Or should she report to the CMO, so that she's in close touch with the other marketers who look after other products and regions? That might make sense if, for example, the company is pivoting from offline to online marketing channels. Then all the marketers involved in that shift can work closely and learn from each other—in which case she should probably be a part of the CMO's team.

But what if her customers in Europe have specific needs that are different from the rest of the world? Then she might be better off reporting to the European MD, enabling her to work super closely with the salespeople who call on those customers. All these options have advantages and disadvantages.

Wherever she reports, in a truly frictionless company, absolutely nothing prevents her from speaking with the people from the other dimensions of the organizational matrix. It's just that, in practice, she's likely to interact with them *less often or less intensively*.

In summary, organizational design is actually a fairly clumsy tool—it's used to allocate decision rights when in many cases decisions will need to be highly collaborative. It can also be used to facilitate situations where people need to interact with each other very frequently, and I find this is the best use of it. But wherever Maya ends up reporting, there will be many people outside that department that she'll need to work with on a regular cadence.

Meeting design is much more fluid and flexible than your formal organizational chart—and a much easier way to orchestrate the right interactions.

Now that we have seen some of the limitations of formal organizational design, let's look at a simpler way of ensuring that the right interactions take place: meeting design.

Get Your Meeting Design Right First

Formal organizational designs are powerful, but they're not very flexible, and they're never perfect. Whatever organizational design you choose involves trade-offs, and the right way to address these trade-offs is through effective meeting design.

By contrast, meeting design is much more fluid and flexible than your formal organizational chart—and a much easier way to orchestrate the right interactions. So, if you're a CEO or CXO in a scaling company, mastering the art of meeting design is a key skill.

Take the case of Maya. She ended up reporting to Sam, the product VP—but she still needed to stay close to the salespeople in the region and the marketing folks in other product divisions. This was easily achieved through effective meeting design, supported by the right information flows.

So, before you head off to do a complete reorganization of your company, ask yourself whether you can get the enhanced performance you need by fine-tuning (or overhauling) your meetings. My experience is that this is very often the case, and it's a much faster and less painful way of getting there. It's only when you haven't been able to solve your coordination and collaboration challenges with the right suite of meetings (and, of course, behaviors) that you might need to take a fresh look at your organizational chart.

Ritual 17:
Designing High-Performance Meetings

Meeting design isn't especially difficult or complex—it just needs to be done with some careful thought—which is not always the case. If you design your meetings with this ritual's approach, then the right people will have the right information and the right interactions to make the right decisions and execute the right things at the right times. It's easy to make adjustments, so you should assess how well they're working at least once per year, and twice if things are changing quickly.

If you're experiencing challenges of coordination or collaboration in your business, meeting design should be the first place you look for a solution. Here are the elements to consider:

- **Pain point:** What is the issue that needs better collaboration or communication?

- **People:** Who needs to be involved?

- **Purpose:** What would the main goal of this meeting be? Is it a decision-making forum, or a forum to coordinate on execution? What needs to be decided or accomplished?

- **Information:** What information will the participants need to achieve the purpose? How will they get it?

- **Cadence:** How often does this meeting need to happen? Is it recurring or ad hoc? If ad hoc, who or what triggers it?

- **Duration:** How long should it last?

- **Stakeholders:** Who needs to be informed about the outcome of the meeting? What information do they need to receive?

Ritual 18:
Clean Up Your Meetings

However good your meetings are today, things change so quickly in high-growth companies that they'll need some regular cleaning up. Use this ritual every six to twelve months to keep your meetings on point, and ask your executives to do the same within their departments. Soon, you'll have a vastly improved suite of meetings, with higher Productivity and Positivity.

Step 1: Map the existing meetings. Have someone collect information about the key meetings that are happening, including both standing ones and important ad hoc ones that tend to recur.

Step 2: Survey the participants. Ask the people who attend these meetings to answer these simple questions:

- Does the meeting have a valuable purpose?
- Is it achieving this purpose?
- Does it consistently focus on important issues?
- Does it have the right participants, supporting information, and frequency?
- Overall, how Productive is this meeting?
- How time-efficient is it?
- How Positive is it?

Step 3: Discuss the results and take appropriate action. Meet with your key executives to review the findings and choose what to do about each meeting:

- Keep: If the meeting is working well, leave it as is.

- Modify: If the meeting is necessary but not working as well as it could, modify its elements (purpose, participants, information, cadence, and stakeholders) to make it more effective.

- Kill: If the meeting doesn't serve an important purpose or is a big time waster, stop having it.

- Create: If there's insufficient communication around an issue or initiative, create a new meeting to bridge that gap.

When to Reorganize

Organizational design is typically not a big concern in the early years—since almost every start-up begins with just one product and one region, they naturally default to a functional structure. But as companies add products and regions, they face the time-old challenge of deciding which of these to make the dominant factor in the organizational design.

For example, Hailey, the CEO of Pacific Grove, had to think about her organizational design when they expanded from one country to two: Should each country have its own head of marketing, sales, and so on, reporting up to the country manager? Or, with only two countries, could one person handle both? She opted for the latter and asked the existing marketing managers to take on the additional responsibility. This worked pretty well, but when they expanded to a third country, that became the trigger to go for a completely different organizational structure.

The other possible trigger is persistent friction. If you're seeing a chronic pattern of poor collaboration or coordination, and nothing seems to help, it may well be time to look at your organizational chart. But first be sure that your challenges are not just a result of relationships, poor interactions, or poor meeting design.

Super-Cart, a company digitizing the retail supply chain in Southeast Asia, had launched many new services in a two-year period but hadn't thought much about whether the organizational design needed to change to support this. After a year of staff working incredibly long hours to make it work, and despite the fact that most people took a very collaborative approach and got along just fine, it wasn't going well. The main complaint was that no one felt they were getting the level of support from product and engineering that they needed. Eventually the CEO realized that something had to change. Both those teams were working as hard as they could, but there was simply no way for them to make the trade-offs between the never-ending demands of multiple internal customers. It was time for a reorganization.

How to Redesign Your Organization

You might think that redesigning an organization requires a specialized consultant with a proven methodology. That's not the case, especially if your head count is in the hundreds, not the thousands. The most successful organizational redesigns I've seen have all been led by the executives who run the company, not by an outside consultant.

There are a few reasons for this. First, no one knows the current pain points better than your management team. Second, every organizational design inevitably comes with trade-offs, and the people who are in the best position to evaluate and make these trade-offs are the executives who will have to live with them. Finally, by making the decisions themselves, executives build more commitment to making the new organizational design work, imperfections and all.

Many CEOs are skeptical of this in-house approach because

they worry that their executives won't be objective when their own empires are at stake. That is, of course, a risk; however, in my experience, it's not nearly as big a factor as you'd think. Most executives are happy to take the "what's best for the company overall" perspective, as long as they're confident that they'll still have a job at the end of it and they don't see others playing politics. In any case, hiring a consultant doesn't protect you from executives who act out of self-interest. Consultants rely on your executives for all their knowledge and insights, and they can easily be influenced by someone selling them a story. By contrast, your other executives can sniff out this kind of self-serving behavior much more easily, so the force of peer pressure combined with effective leadership by the CEO is usually enough to prevent political behavior from derailing this process.

Redesign Your Organization

Because I explicitly *don't* want you to reorganize your company regularly, I'm not calling this a ritual. But I'll provide a brief guide to how to go about it when the time comes.

To lead a reorganization discussion, all you need to do is gather a group of four to six trusted senior executives. Sit together over a few sessions and run through the following steps:

Step 1: Clarify your strategy and your must-win battles.

Step 2: Identify the current pain points in the organizational structure—especially those that are interfering with your execution on the must-win battles.

Step 3: Start to brainstorm a range of new organizational structure options. Be creative and don't evaluate them at this stage!

Step 4: Hold a quick vote to pick the top two or three options.

Then spend some time refining each of them further.

Step 5: Create a list of the key advantages and drawbacks for each option.

Step 6: Consider how meeting design can overcome some of the drawbacks of your preferred option or options. I often find that a preferred solution falls out at this point—since in many (but not all) cases, effective meeting design can compensate for the drawbacks of a given design. From here on out, you should think about the process as one of ongoing refinement.

Step 7: Now is the time to involve a broader group of executives in the process. Engage the next layer of executives in small working groups. Share your current best option or options, what you're confident about, and what concerns remain, then ask for their input and suggestions. Hopefully you'll be able to fine-tune the design and gain buy-in over the course of a few such discussions.

Step 8: Evaluate, decide, and start planning the implementation and communication of your strategy.

Create an Organizational Road Map

A core theme running through this book is that leaders of high-growth companies often fail to anticipate the demands that growth will place on their organization. This leads to frictions that only get senior management's attention when they've become a real problem, by which time they're much harder to address. Major reorganizations such as the one Super-Cart had to go through are painful and slow you down, so they are to be avoided if at all possible.

Much better is to make smaller, more frequent adjustments as you go. This means anticipating the changes that will be needed before they turn into big problems so that you can plan and implement these changes in a more frictionless way. This requires a road map.

Ritual 19:
Create an Organizational Road Map

Think about how much energy digital companies invest in their product road map. They spend a huge amount of time on this, involving multiple senior executives. Why? Because product evolution involves a lot of complexity, so it's essential to have a clear plan that integrates multiple views. The same is true for your evolving organization. In fact, building a product road map and an organizational road map are very similar processes. That's why it's important to do your very best to think, anticipate, and plan for the organization you'll need in the future—and that's what this ritual is about.

Step 1: Gather the right participants. Once a year, gather a group of people who can help you to think through where the company is going and how that will translate into the organization you will need in the future to be successful. Ideally, this group should include not only your top executives but also one or two board members or advisors who have been through scaling journeys in similar companies. You may also want to bring in a consultant or coach to help guide the process.

Step 2: Look two years down the road. What are your goals for business growth and expansion? What new products do you expect to launch? How many more customers will you have? In what countries? How will you support them? What is the competition up to, and how will you need to respond? How is regulation changing? What new challenges will you face? Try to describe all the key changes that you can foresee, even in your administrative and support functions.

Step 3: Consider which of these changes are likely to have the biggest implications for your organization, and focus on those. Some parts of your organization may scale organically as your company grows; others may need to change dramatically. Think about whether the changes you foresee in your business are likely to require incremental changes in your organizational capabilities and processes or more drastic changes, and zoom in on those areas where significant change is likely.

Step 4: Identify the capabilities you'll need two years out, and do a gap analysis. What capabilities will you need to be successful at that point? Compare these to those you have today; then bucket them as follows:

- **New:** Capabilities that you'll need to build from scratch (or acquire).

- **Broken:** Capabilities you have today that aren't even meeting your current needs well (and therefore are definitely not good enough for your future requirements).

- **Not scalable:** Capabilities you have that are working well enough today, but aren't likely to scale to meet your future needs, so will need some kind of retooling or development.

- **Good to go:** Capabilities you have today that meet your current needs *and* should be able to scale to meet future needs.

Step 5: Work backward to build a road map. What will it take to get your organization from where it is to where it needs to be in two years? Your road map should ideally consider the following factors:

- What type of people to hire, at what level, and when.

- How you will integrate these new hires.

- How your organizational structure will need to be altered to encompass them.

- What systems or processes may need to be built or modified to support this scaling.

Then divide these into steps that need to be taken today, versus those that can wait three, six, nine, twelve months, or longer. If you don't have the resources or bandwidth to tackle everything, discuss which are the key ones to invest in.

Step 6: Allocate responsibilities. Finally, ask yourself who will be responsible for executing each step in the road map and how you'll hold the team accountable for progress.

Once you've created the road map, it should be a living tool that you and your team refer back to as you implement these initiatives. It will certainly change over time, and that's okay. But hopefully your road map will prevent you from getting slowed down by unforeseen organizational change needs.

Still One Company

We've talked about architecting interactions through meeting design as well as formal organizational structure, but the leadership team also plays a role in facilitating informal interactions. This can happen in all kinds of ways, including office design, parties, offsites, town halls, and more. These are all fairly straightforward, and most companies do them pretty well.

So, let's focus on one area where many start-ups struggle. As your company gets large, many staff inevitably lose touch with what other parts of the business are up to and what's happening beyond their own team or department. This typically shows up in engagement surveys either as a complaint that they don't know what's happening or a request for more updates. But when companies respond with newsletters, a new intranet, or other company-wide communications, they are almost invariably ignored by most staff. Now you're supplying the information they asked for, but suddenly there is no demand for it! What to do?

Ritual 20:
Run an Information Marketplace

This ritual addresses the dilemma of keeping your staff informed as to what's going on in your company—without spoon-feeding them to the point that they switch off. The solution is to create a *marketplace* that matches supply and demand for information about the company. If you run this ritual every three to six months, it helps build and maintain meaningful connections across different parts of the company and keep everyone feeling that they're "still one company" and that they know what's going on.

Step 1: Choose a handful of areas or topics to highlight.
These can be a department, a team, a new product, a recent acquisition, or any important initiative. Ask a leader from that area to create a short presentation about what they're doing, how it connects to the rest of the company, what will be happening in the coming months, and who is on their team. Explain that the idea is to create a very informal conversation, so leaders should present their area for no more than ten minutes, leaving the rest of the time for Q&A and informal discussions.

223

Step 2: Schedule a virtual or in-person conference. Block off two to three hours for the event. Divide the time into thirty-minute blocks. You'll want to run four to six chat rooms in parallel, one for each of the topics you've chosen. But make sure you have more topics than there are time slots— say, six to eight topics for four slots. That forces employees to *choose* which sessions to join, which changes their state of mind from "I have to go to this" to "I'm interested in hearing about this." Leave five minutes between blocks for people to have a quick break.

Step 3: Run the event. Limit the sign-up for each chat room based on how many people you need to accommodate—I find, twelve is a good number, but it can be up to twenty.

Step 4: Finish the event. If you can run the event in person, now's a great time to hold a party! If it's online, a good idea is to use the last thirty-minute block for a town hall. These events give your people a chance to interact with leaders they wouldn't normally meet and to learn about areas they may not know much about. Because staff choose their own topics and hear about them in an intimate and interactive session, they'll come out of these sessions feeling much more connected to the rest of the company.

Most of the friction growth companies experience boils down to the quality of their people's interactions, which has been our focus throughout most of this book. But to make the most of the dialogue skills you've learned, it pays to make sure the right interactions are taking place. Organizational and meeting design have a massive influence on who talks to whom, how often, and about what. Even if all your interactions are Productive and Positive, if crucial ones are missing, it will hold your company back.

In this chapter, you've learned three rituals for architecting those interactions at different levels. The Create an Organizational Road Map Ritual (page 220) helps you identify the best structure for your organization and plan how it will evolve to support the business. The Clean Up Your Meetings Ritual (page 215) ensures that you create the right cross-functional connections to balance the trade-offs you made in your organizational design. Finally, the Run an Information Marketplace Ritual (page 223) helps people across the organization get a sense of the whole and stay informed about what's happening in other parts of the company.

These rituals don't need to happen very often. But even though you only need them occasionally, they play an essential role in keeping your company operating at peak performance.

Recap

- CEOs should think about organizational design as a way of enabling effective communications, as well as a way of allocating decision rights.

- But before you turn to organizational design, you should evaluate whether you can achieve your goals and solve problems through improved meeting design.

- Even if there are no acute organizational problems, it pays to have a good look at the effectiveness of your main meetings from time to time, as they are a powerful driver of Productivity and Positivity.

- Organizational redesign is more likely to be necessary when adding new products or geographies, or when frictions persist.

- Organizational design should be led by key executives and not outsourced to a consultant.

- Frequent small adjustments to an organization are preferable to major reorganizations, which inevitably cause a lot of lost productivity.

- Information marketplaces can help your people stay feeling connected to the company as a whole, even as it grows.

Chapter 14

Ready . . . Set . . . Scale

▼

EVERY ORGANIZATION DEVELOPS FRICTION as it scales. That's just life. It's okay.

What's not okay is to do nothing about it.

One simple fact makes tackling this a lot easier than you might imagine: *your people already know where the frictions are* in your organization. They know which decisions are getting bogged down in bureaucracy or politics. Which meetings are a waste of time. Which managers aren't giving clear direction to their people. Which teams are dysfunctional. Which groups can't get along with each other. Who is bad-mouthing whom. All the knowledge you need to identify these dysfunctions is already there, in your organization.

Your people already know where the frictions are in your organization.

Your first step is accessing this knowledge. That's all about creating a culture of trust where people aren't scared to name what's going on. Remember, *you can't solve the problem if you can't discuss it, and you can't discuss it if you can't name it*. But as scary as it may seem at the outset, you'll soon find that when you name these (bucket 2) issues, everyone actually relaxes. Why? Because they've known about it all along—and they've gossiped about it at the bar—but now they see that the organization is prepared to do something about it. Name what's actually going on a few times, and the fear soon subsides.

Your next step is to help your people get comfortable having "us" conversations. The best way to do so is by role modeling—when they see you and your coleaders doing it, they'll quickly catch on. You should also lean on rituals like Share Your Personal User Guide (page 97) and Contracting for Feedback (page 130), which provide a structured framework for having "us" conversations in a safe and constructive way.

Once you've created a culture that recognizes the importance of dealing with "us" issues and feels comfortable doing so, you're in a position to prevent future frictions from developing. This is where the rest of the rituals come in.

As a leader, it's your job to create an organization in which your people can do their best work, achieve their goals, build high-trust relationships, be part of high-performing teams, and love coming to work every day. Those outcomes are driven by the quality of their interactions. Which brings us back to the two-eyed CEO: the idea that, while you must always keep one eye firmly on the "it" issues, you should keep the other on "us" issues, such as the quality of your people's interactions and the factors that support or undermine them.

Naturally, not all leaders are equally good at this task. Perhaps you're at heart an innovator or a technologist, or you're more product oriented than people oriented. Maybe your EQ and OQ just aren't that strong. That's okay—if you lean on the rituals, they'll get you a long way.

You should also elevate the people in your organization who do have these skills: make sure they have a seat at the table. Give them a voice. Ask them, "How is our organization doing? What do we need to pay attention to?" Just as you don't need to be a finance whiz to run a company with strong financial processes, you don't need to be great at mastering frictions yourself—but you do need to give it a place of importance.

If there's one idea that justifies your commitment to this path, it's this: *Productivity and Positivity are inextricably intertwined.* You can never achieve consistently high Productivity for your company unless your people have high-quality interactions, which is where Positivity is generated or destroyed. The factors that drive Positivity are not difficult to understand. People want to feel understood. They want to be treated with respect. They want to feel that their voice matters and that they have influence. And they want to know that when tensions or problems arise, they'll be addressed and resolved in a healthy way, not left to fester. These conditions unleash your people's commitment, motivation, creativity, and teamwork.

Imagine that you started down this path and a few years have passed. Your company now has hundreds, maybe thousands, of employees, and everyone is *still* Thinking Together (page 55), still sharing their PUGs (page 97), and still Turning Tensions into Trust (page 101). Teams are still running great Deep-Dive Meetings (page 143) and sharing feedback with other teams (page 174). Even though your organization is vastly more complex, the quality of interactions remains consistently high, which helps everyone do their best work and feel good about it.

You've successfully achieved smooth scaling.

I encourage you to feel confident that all of this is per-fectly doable. Your organization's frictions can be resolved and prevented, and that *will* inexorably lead to improved performance—as well as a healthier culture. In short, the virtuous cycle has begun.

Acknowledgments

∨

I WOULD LIKE TO ACKNOWLEDGE two great thinkers and writers whose work has had the most influence on my own.

Nancy Kline, the founder of Time to Think and creator of The Thinking Environment, has been an inspiration to me, and her work has informed much of mine. Her extraordinary clarity of thought is matched only by the elegance and simplicity of her methods and her warmth as a person.

I was lucky enough to study under Professor Chris Argyris (deceased) of the Harvard Business School and Yale School of Management. I have yet to encounter a better diagnostician of what goes wrong in organizations, and his training opened my eyes to what was happening below the surface in the companies I served.

A big hug full of thanks to Madison Fitzpatrick, my coblogger and writing coach. Your infectious enthusiasm and easy laughter made the ten days we spent assembling the manuscript on a Bali hilltop a delight.

A huge thanks to Maggie Langrick and the entire crew at Wonderwell for your support and belief in the project, your hard work, and the much-needed structure and discipline you provided.

To my clients, I thank all of you for having had trust in me and allowing me into the inner sanctum of your organizations.

About the Author

❯

ROB BIER IS A SEASONED EXPERT in building high-performance organizations, with more than twenty years' experience in the field. He has helped over 40 scale-ups, start-ups, and growth companies to scale successfully, including six that became unicorns or decacorns during the time he partnered with them.

He is the driving force behind Trellis Partners, a firm that supports entrepreneurs and senior business leaders on scaling-related issues, including leadership, teams, culture, and execution.

Previously he was the founder and CEO of Sparck (a fin-tech acquired by Citigroup), cofounder and CEO of venture capital firm Antfactory, and a senior partner in the Organizational Performance practice of Monitor Group (now Monitor Deloitte). He also served on the Management Advisory Board of TowerBrook Capital Partners.

Rob earned an engineering degree from Stanford and an MBA from Harvard. He enjoys classic cars, cooking, hiking, tennis, travel, and hanging out with his kids. He currently resides in Singapore with his two dogs, Hoffmann and Rosie Bagel. Learn more at robbier.com.